I0120300

SWEPT UP IN
HATE

A STUDY OF THE CAUSES AND OUTCOMES
OF ANTI-SEMITISM

Why is it that humans turn to hate?
How did Anti-Semitism develop?
A comprehensive opinion study of causes and outcomes!

Isaac Zelazny

Braughler™
Books

Copyright © 2022 by Isaac Zelazny. All rights reserved.

The views and opinions expressed in this work are those of the author and do not necessarily reflect the views and opinions of Braughler Books LLC.

This book or any portion thereof may not be reproduced or used in any manner whatsoever without the express written permission of the publisher except for the use of brief quotations in a scholarly work or book review. For permissions or further information contact Braughler Books LLC at: info@braughlerbooks.com.

Cover photo: ID 29582446 © mpz | 123RF

Printed in the United States of America
Published by Braughler Books LLC., Springboro, Ohio
First printing, 2022
ISBN: 978-1-955791-49-6

Library of Congress Control Number: 2022921463

Ordering information: Special discounts are available on quantity purchases by bookstores, corporations, associations, and others. For details, contact the publisher at: sales@braughlerbooks.com or at 937-58-BOOKS

For questions or comments about this book, please write to:
info@braughlerbooks.com

Braughler™
Books
braughlerbooks.com

About the author

Isaac is a retired Jet engine engineer. His formal education is in the Engineering sciences. However, as a side interest, Isaac has been studying topics dealing with humanity, history, cultures, religions, mythology and human justice topics.

In addition, both parents and grandparents survived the holocaust perpetuated by Nazi Germany and their collaborators on European Jews in particular and others broadly. Isaac has extensively discussed their personal experiences during the Holocaust. As a child, he was always intrigued by discussions regarding events during World War Two.

Isaac was also a docent and often a speaker at the National Museum of the United States Air Force in Dayton Ohio as well as other venues on the topic of the Holocaust.

Isaac had many international work assignments in different countries. In addition to residing in those places, Isaac has traveled the world extensively and has been a student of cultures and the histories of each country and region visited.

CONTENTS

INTRODUCTION

Why did I write this book?

There is a noticeable rise in hate acts, hate speech and Anti-Semitism (anti-Jewish) sentiments in particular. Acts of racism and xenophobia (fear of outsiders) in general is carried out in the open and in full display. It has become overt and at times it is even been advertised and livestreamed on the internet in real time by the perpetrators.

Not only is it perpetuated by individuals and organizations, it has now penetrated some governments around the world which have tied Nationalism to being under attack by Jews, immigrants and anyone that does not look like them.

Anti-Jewish sentiment was always there since Christianity formed 2000 years ago. This book will attempt to study how it formed and how it is perpetuated. The attempt here is to educate especially the vulnerable and impressionable younger generation so as to not have events repeated, perpetuated, tolerated or participate in it.

This book compiles the many aspects that have contributed to this unique form of hate and provides a personal experience from my grandparents, parents, extended family and myself.

Obviously, this is a controversial topic especially when conversing with folks from other religions that wholesale deny it exists as an institution, or worse, that Jews deserve it.

Only by exposing the horrors of the past, showing it to our young that they too may be victims if they are ambivalent to it, will the horrors of these unjust acts be avoided or at least minimized. The resultant of the term "Never again" will remain a slogan, a statement and basically fade away unless the message is shared and acted upon.

Even though my last chapter talks about a solution, the sad reality is that it is so engrained, that in many circles this can't be addressed or remedied. In addition to education, the preservation of a Jewish land in Israel will provide the only safe harbor for Jews. When that is threatened, a repeat of attacks on Jews and the possibility of another holocaust can't be ignored.

Lastly, and related to it, is the Israeli-Palestinian conflict. That conflict has devolved into religious and ethnic inspired years of wars, death and destruction. While, I will not delve too deeply into that topic in this book, it too has accelerated worldwide Anti-Jewish sentiments and personal attacks on the innocent. Those conflicts are residual tribal thinking in which every side believes they have exclusive rights to the lands (and God is always on their side; what else? (sarcastic)).

The advent of the fall of the Turkish Ottoman Empire after World War One, the subsequent British and French takeover of the Middle East for the purpose of natural resources exploitation and the creation of artificial borders that separated people, just added to the mix of hate and endless wars. But that is a topic of another book.

THE APPROACH USED FOR THIS STUDY

There are multiple ways of approaching a topic. Initially I was tempted to scientifically write the chapters and provide detailed evidence to each point. However, that is not attainable by me and would immediately be challenged on every minutia with a counter argument. While discussion and details are important, the message of Anti-Semitism will be lost in the details because it is so prevalent and ever consumed by deniers and revisionists.

The book does not claim to be a definitive narrative, opinion nor absolute as I rely mainly on a variety of public sources of information and personal observations including from people that were directly impacted by acts of Anti-Semitism.

Instead of using a textbook approach to the topic, I will use informational format and infuse with personal observations and material that is generally studied, available or observed. As my personal historical interest in this topic, I will provide my insight at every step. Textual citing will be provided where it can be obtained, as well as information that was gathered over the years.

Please note that this study does not attempt to quote every word and sentence nor can it be used as absolute, but rather provide the reader with broad material as seen from the perspective of the persecuted. Since we are dealing with Anti-Jewish acts and sentiments, you will see it from the perspective of a non-practicing Jewish person (me).

The book may be considered as an opinion piece. It deals with a non-solvable situation on a world scale and I am sure there are people who will argue the opposite or at worse that we Jews deserve it all (yes it was said to me directly). Then there are religious zealots that will point out that this is "God's will" and it is a prophesy and it is part of the religious journey of Jews (all of which is nonsense hateful trash talking).

I would propose the notion that when Jews are left out of politics and religious self-righteous, fear mongering, and self-centered provocateurs, that the probability of violence will be greatly reduced.

The hate of Jews is like no other group hate! The Jews have been under attack for thousands of years and probably thousands more to come since it is so engrained in teachings of those wishing Jews to be eliminated at worse, or converted at best.

Chapter's flow

I decided to cluster chapters together to address specific areas and allow the reader to see various aspects of that topic. Each of these clusters could be further studied on their own, or together for a particular need. The reader can even skip around if there is a specific interest (I suggest you do it after reading the entire book) and even enhance that experience with your own. Some material is repeated in the various sections to emphasize a point. That is not an oversight, but rather a method of returning to the points where hatred of Jews started from. This method will also allow me to expand each topic and allows for a continuation and further updates to this book..

The first cluster of chapters deals with the basic human trait leading to hate and how it is further develops into institutionalized hate.

PART I: WHY WE HATE
Chapter 1: Why Hate
Chapter 2: Why Loyalty
Chapter 3: Sacrifice
Chapter 4: Systems of Conformity

The second cluster of chapters deals with how other major religions view Jews and institutionalize hate and collective punishment.

PART II: ROLE OF RELIGIONS IN HATE
Chapter 5: Religion as Forms of Institutions
Chapter 6: The Role of Religion in Hate
Chapter 7: Early Christianity
Chapter 8: The Islamic World and Jews

The next two section of chapters deals with the definition Jews and then of Anti-Semitism. I then go further in time to describe biblical Jews because Anti-Semitism, Anti-Jewish

PART III: WHO IS A JEW
Chapter 9: Biblical Jews
Chapter 10: Who is a Jew

sentiments have occurred early on and are mentioned in the bible such as the forced Hellenization (Greek culture) on Jews/Hebrews that included conversion.

Next, we deal with 19th and 20th century massive change in which hate manifests itself with genocide of Jews that led to the Holocaust. I then address the aftermath in which the perpetrators, their enablers and Anti-Semites use the power of "free Speech" to subvert the truth by denials, manipulate the message of hate and outright justify it.

The next cluster of chapters deal with primary 20th century contributors to Anti-Semitism as well as the progression of hate that penetrated American politics in particular, but not exclusively.

In these chapters, I deal with the consequences of conversion away from Judaism and also, the inadvertent affects that some in the Atheist community in contributing to hate directed at Jews.

The last section will provide my personal experiences and direct insights. And finally, a solution that may address some, but in reality, if it is deeply rooted as I described, it cannot change minds that are already set in hate!

PART I: WHY WE HATE

CHAPTER 1

Why Hate

Introduction to the topic

Since the beginning of time, humans tended to separate themselves into smaller groups for primary purposes of protection. As an observer of nature, you can actually see it in many living beings. The difference however, is that as thinking humans, we are able to go further and rationalize events and outcomes to suit the results or intended results. Today, the advent of fast-moving information flow offered by the internet accelerates this process in the form of shared opinions, lessons learned and the perpetuation of group think in a non-personal means and even remotely. This book attempts to point out the specifics of hate, hate speech, Anti-Semitism and their historical consequences.

Hate—How did it form

Humans have a self-preservation mechanism that goes beyond Fight or Flight mode that is ingrained into our biological makeup. The fight or flight is a mechanism in which when a person (or an animal) is under physical attack can subconsciously choose to fight the attacker or if there is a hope of avoiding a fight or the inability to fight back overwhelming attacker, choose to flee or run away. These are primal ways in which humans have acted upon. As small groups succeeded in the protection of their lives and food sources, the next step was the protection of property. Early form of property was usually grazing animals, sources of food and tools, and yes, females for the purpose of procreation. As accumulation of property increased, humans looked up to a leader for direction and means of protecting what's theirs. A leader was tasked with the selection of where to live, where to gather food/hunt... The price that a leader exacted on the group was obedience, deference, unquestioning loyalty. All wrapped up in what we call "respect." Respect however, has many manifestations. What some people define respect as being polite, being accepting, being gracious. However, Respect is also interpreted by those who are leaders as an unquestioned conformity

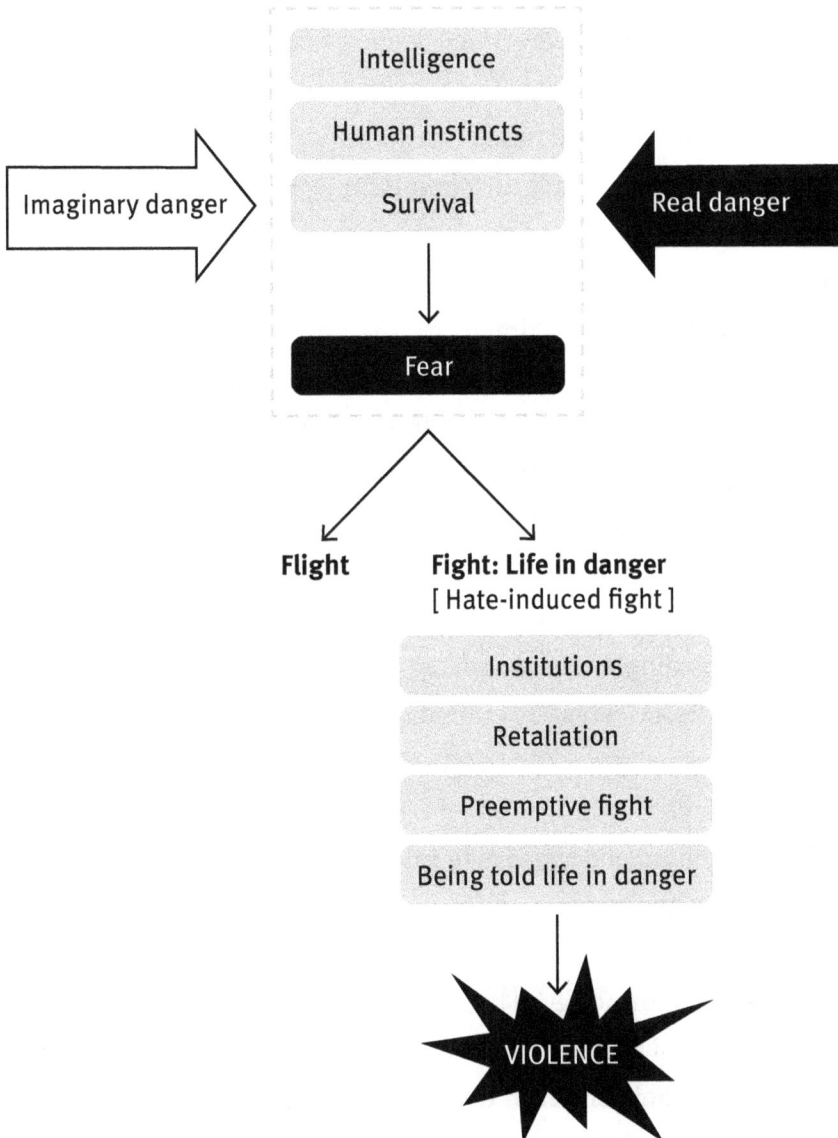

```
                    ┌─────────────────────────┐
                    │      Intelligence        │
                    │                          │
                    │    Human instincts       │
  ⇨ Imaginary danger│       Survival           │ ◀ Real danger
                    │          │               │
                    │          ▼               │
                    │        Fear              │
                    └──────────┬──────────────┘
                          ↙         ↘
                      Flight    Fight: Life in danger
                                [ Hate-induced fight ]

                                  Institutions
                                  Retaliation
                                  Preemptive fight
                                Being told life in danger
                                        │
                                        ▼
                                    ✦ VIOLENCE ✦
```

Hate induces fear/Fear induces hate. Both bring on violence.

15

and loyalty to the leader. The leaders and their entourage needed to create systems of conformity. In other words, instead of demanding loyalty from each person in the group in a direct way, they devised a method in which a system being created will have the group conform in totality as well as individually.

The easiest way to control a mass of people is to subdivide the group by creating hierarchy or casts. This system is a pyramid of importance in which the leader is on top (usually a male). Below the leader are close confidants and sub leaders loyal to the king and willing to enforce his bidding. Below that are the more operational leaders tasked with carrying the leader's agenda. Lower still are the "lieutenants" that control the "foot soldiers" to control and administers punishments in a public spectacle in order to intimidate the population into submission. The ordinary people were always on the bottom and had no say in matters.

But...

You needed to add legitimacy to this process or else, any person can challenge the leader on a whim and try to depose them.

Why legitimacy? Well, that is simple! It taps into the human fear of the unknown. It taps into humans not understanding their surroundings or natural events and thus created deities and gods to explain it all. The mere fact that the ordinary human feels vulnerable when not in control, they enlist these "fear created gods." And because the gods are sometimes vengeful, angry, demanding, humans created a conduit to these gods. Those conduits were priests, priestesses, shamans, sages.... To add to the aura of legitimacy, only those priests could talk to the gods. And the gods only talked to their "chosen ones."

The next phase of control is to interweave those conduits to the gods into their hierarchy. That by itself created the illusion of "legitimacy." After all, the messages were always that the "gods will it" and thus it is their will whether you like it or not. And because humans are a fearful sort (remember the saying I will put the "Fear of God into you" as routinely invoked by some parents to their children discipline? Here is another term: "he is a god-fearing Christian"?).

Now you got the system of control, you weave into it the gods (really the priests) and you got a perfect system of subjugation. And because only the priests talk to their gods, they actually got to select the next leader because god "anointed" that future leader (whether the leader is a king, or tribal leader, the end result is the same). You routinely hear about European monarchs "chosen by God himself." That is the legitimacy components that most subjects accept blindly. To bring some current perspective to it, during the last US presidential election (in 2020) you would hear from Christian leaders that "Trump was anointed by God" and thus it is God's will for him to be the president faults and all. And since God is perfect and makes no mistakes, there is a purpose for that leader to be in that position and thus obedience is "legitimized again."

And while there, let me digress a bit. Did you notice that when wedding vows are exchanged (in many circles), it is the wife that must declare her obedience to her husband? And it is not mutual. The man's obedience is to God. Thus, a small hierarchy is created at home as well. All these are designed to keep the population at check for the purpose of control. This connection to divinity allows man (as in the gender) to completely take over and basically do what they want. Multiple wives are just the beginning. In many religions and cultures, the hierarchy is the same. God on top (or whatever deity is selected), then the King (or tribal leader), then the priests, then the leadership and lastly the poor peasants (or the rest of the population).

CHAPTER 2

Why Loyalty

Humans created groups, tribes, clans for the purpose of self-preservation and protection. In order to identify themselves visually, each created dress codes that are unique and easy to recognize. Humans then created religions and rituals (gods and deities). All are built upon the internal human fear of the unknown. Then as these segregations evolved, leaders were selected or emerged thru violence or necessity, but that did not come freely as they demanded obedience and ultimately payments. How can control over the members be preserved?

What is Loyalty?

Loyalty is the means in which a leader (or leadership) can assure himself/itself of common goal sharing at the most, complicity/support and at worse, a non-interference (or counter effort). Again, loyalty is a form of control in which the leader does not participate in a physical control or challenging action. Loyalty is the expected nonviolent aspect of power retention. However, the consequences of disloyalty are almost always executed by others in the group and range from verbal retribution, shunning, banning, exile, physical torture and death (usually in public to set an example). Another form of the consequences of disloyalty (real or perceived), is the punishment of that person's family, neighbors and as communities grew, an entire people.

Evolution of loyalty

Within a primitive and ever evolving community, a leader emerged and established themselves via loyalty and allegiance, there was a need to enlarge the group in order to increase the wealth and fortunes of the entire community as a whole and the leader/leadership foremost. Remember, that the price of leadership is the taking of material from others and accumulating it for the purpose of getting things done by mutual means. A leader basically rationalizes the accumulation of wealth as "I give you leadership, direction, keep you alive with my decisions and protection, and in turn I get things such as property, wives, animals, objects of value and the storage of food." The problem of wealth accumulation by the leadership is that often their plans exceed their means and thus physical confiscation of other possessions was created.

Unless leaders are able or willing to trade, they formed raiding parties and took from the next tribe. At its height, this form of "grabbing" from others manifested itself in colonialism. No longer were leaders satisfied with their little group or tribe, they created empires of physical proportions as well as cultural/religious empires.

Loyalty was also demanded by the prevailing religions. The common way of demanding loyalty from the common people was in the form of taxes. Taxes were also used to finance militaries that would go out and conquer others. Additionally, loyalty was exacted in the form of conscription in which young men were forced to serve in the military sometimes for as long as 20 years (assuming they were still alive and able) before they were allowed to return to their villages or towns.

Loyalty is also a perverted test to see if a person can be trusted or removed by a leader. Loyalty tests always are followed by purges and executions (Night of the Long Knives in Nazi Germany, Joseph Stalin's murderous purges in the Soviet Union, or Saddam Hussein rise to power in Iraq).

A classic Loyalty test excuse directed against Jews can be demonstrated by the French military accusing captain Alfred Dreyfus of treason.[1] Here is a French military person having Jewish heritage being falsely accused of treason and made an example in public.

Loyalty test is a two-edged sword and will cut both ways. However, it is still demanded to this day and any opposition to it is deemed unpatriotic, treasonous, disloyal.

As an aside, allegiance is related to loyalty, but is designed to work in a pluralistic or democratic society, where loyalty is demanded primarily in a monarchy or dictatorship, it is done to the person and not to the country or people.

When you hear "Hail Caesar," or "Heil Hitler," it is a mark of loyalty to that person. When you pledge allegiance, you do it for the country or institution (Constitution) and not the leader. However, in a perverted mind there is no difference when the leader combines the two. Then the followers think they can be both loyal to the person and the Constitution. This is a scenario where the Constitution is highjacked, manipulated and becomes secondary to loyalty of that said leader.

What is happening is that whomever controls the media, has access to daily misinformation and propaganda and if it is fed constantly, the simple-minded audience starts to believe in it. Today, the media is so fragmented that it may not be easy to separate real from made up. Many do not bother and just tune in to what they are programed to.

CHAPTER 3

Sacrifice

Enter the power and the use of sacrifice.

The road to hate

Early cults and religions relied on the good fortune bestowed upon them by these gods, deities and forces of nature. "I need my crops to succeed, I want to prevent famine in my land, I want the plague to go away, I want more children...." That reliance on the supernatural meant there is a price to pay. Nothing is for nothing as the saying goes. The gods always demanded something from you and they will in return may give you what you are asking for (maybe, since the gods are fickle and mischievous).

Forms of payments to curry favors

Food:

Early form of payment was usually food offerings. Simple alters were built and offerings were made to the gods and favors were asked. If those were "accepted," you were granted your wishes and went on your way happy.

Sacrifice part 1—Death for life

Demands and the request got bigger, and the "rejection rate" by the gods got more prevalent, a need for a greater payment was perceived and perpetuated by the intermediaries such as priests and shamans. That payment was then escalated in value by a taking of a life or a blood sacrifice. Early sacrifices consisted of killing of animals. Initially small animals such as birds or small mammals.

Sacrifice part 2- Greater death for life and property

Later on, when those small sacrifices were not deemed sufficient, the sacrifice of larger animals was demanded. Goats, sheep, cows, buffalos, pigs etc.... When individual slaughter of an animal was not sufficient, multiple animals were sacrificed. It goes on today in some cultures.

Sacrifice part 3—Ultimate death for life.

Those gods and deities were very finicky and demanded ever greater sacrifices in order to grant the wishes of the requestor. Those demands were always at the behest of priests. In some cases, a person stated a direct line of communication with a gods (as in Greek or Nordic mythology, and later in biblical texts). That ultimate sacrifice was the killing of a close person that was either from the group or direct relation of the requestor themselves (such as a son or daughter). There was a perception that the swapping of a life for a cause was needed and thus justified. Examples of those sacrifices are demonstrated in early texts, art works, biblical writing and mythology. In Greek mythology, Andromeda, the daughter of the Aethiopian king Cepheus and his wife Cassiopeia, is chained to a rock as a sacrifice to be devoured by a sea monster (luckily, she was saved by Perseus). Or during the Trojan wars, Iphigenia was a daughter of the Greek king Agamemnon and was sacrificed in order to achieve victory and garner the support of the goddess Athena. In biblical terms, Abraham was told by God to sacrifice his son Isaac as a sign of a covenant and loyalty (that was ultimately "downgraded" to body mutilation in the form of a circumcision). However, Abraham later sacrificed a ram to please God.

Sacrifice part 4—Death of others in the community

As death sacrifices of a kin or a leader relatives fell out of favor, the modification became sacrificing other people from the community under the pretense that it is needed to preserve the society. This was common in some

Forms of sacrifice

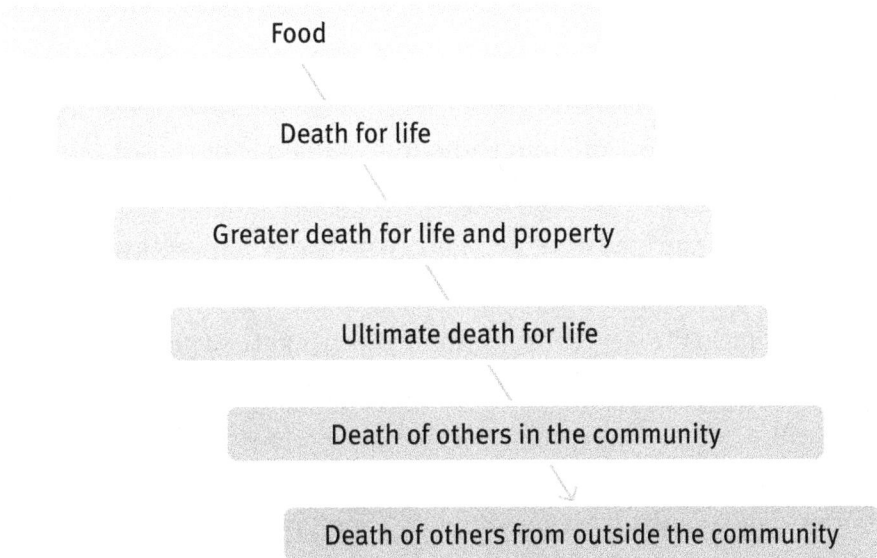

Food

Death for life

Greater death for life and property

Ultimate death for life

Death of others in the community

Death of others from outside the community

cultures like Maya and Aztec in Central and South America. But that too was not a favorite way of appeasing the gods.

Sacrifice part 5—death of others from outside the community.
A further modification of human sacrifices was the capture of outsiders for the sole purpose of appeasement to the gods. Raiding parties were formed and went into neighboring territories and by force taking individuals to be hauled back and later sacrificed on alters. The advantage that was rationalized is that the gods did not care which human is sacrificed, so why not sacrifice someone you do not know? This aspect became the sacrifice of an individual. Their death was nothing more than a trade, a barter and the sacrificial person is nothing more than a commodity.

Note that this form of sacrifice was not considered a retribution or punishment. It merely became a "practical" outcome of getting to favorable results for those that practiced rituals in which they ceded power to the gods.

Retribution and blame deaths.

The next phase and one that started the practice of hate killing is the whole-sale murder and killing because they did not conform, or did not contribute (in the form of taxes, levies, protection money or other demands). Clear evidence of retribution and punishment for religious purposes were seen (or at least purported ones). Early Greeks demanded Jews eat pork during their occupation of the land of Israel. Then you mix in empires aspirations and a whole people are punished as during the Jews revolt against the Romans culminating in the siege, enslavement and ultimate suicide at Masada in the Judean desert. Or the story of uprising by Spartacus and his co-gladiators during the Roman empire days. Entire group was slaughtered, killed by crucifixion or sold into slavery.

Those massacres were perpetuated by the ruling kings for the purposes of conformity to preserve wealth by the rulers. Any one resisting in anyway was considered a threat (real or created) and thus a "punishment was in order." The idea of going into a foreign land and killing the inhabitants for the express purpose of a cultural and religious elimination was not yet developed in early days of human civilization. There were massacres that were part of a master plan to conquer that land. Propaganda existed to spread the message that the perpetuator's attacking force is actually doing the saving of a way of life back home. That kind of propaganda required a lot of resources and organization.

CHAPTER 4

Systems of Conformity and Loyalty

OK, so the leaders and their immediate supporters understood that you just cannot force each member of their group to simply conform just because someone said so. Also, it was too risky to have members always "fight it out" like animals do to gain dominance. For example: a male lion fights another lion for domination of the pride. Same with many other animals in which an Alpha animal is a result of physical confrontation. The problem of physical confrontation is that often it results in serious injury or death to both. Even small altercations and fights within the animal groups can result in an injury to the Alpha leader.

As thinking beings, the advent of systems and institutions were devised and created to protect the leadership from harm and ensure dominance and succession with minimum chance of harm to themselves. Of course, that is not always the way events worked. Many kings were notorious fighters such as the Greek king Alexander "The Great," however, that has become more an exception. The "dirty" task of eliminating opponents were relegated to assassins or loyalists or institutions.

Institutions.

Now that we understand the why, let's look at where did it go from there.

Since humans have a basic trait of protection they share with other animals, the idea of a group a tribe or a clan has emerged. In order for a tribe to function well, you need all to follow without question or else too many opinions will pull the tribe in different directions (democracy has always been difficult to maintain and dictatorship usually follows chaos and dis-function). The problem with multiple opinions is that the decision-making process is lengthy and the outcome may be too late (such as how to pro-tect the group from an imminent attack). In some cases, different opinions result in what we call "in-fighting" or in the past few centuries what we call Civil wars.

A way to mitigate in-fighting is to create a culture that identifies all the members of that group. A culture is created via language, art, music, rituals and most importantly an outward appearance in the form of clothing, hair style, gestures such as body language and hand signs as well as body pierc-ing/mutilations/ scarring, body painting and tattoos. All are designed to let both the group members and outsiders know that this particular individual belongs to a group (like the Japanese Yakuza). Lately though, tattoos have become a billboard for personal statements.

For the members all those symbols are psychologically comforting signs that their well-being is not under attack because members of the same group do not prey on each other. A member walks around outside their immediate territory, they will look for others sharing their "marking" as a quick visual to garner support, protection or common interests. All that external symbolism is needed before two individuals or groups meet in order to assess if that other is a threat, or have the ability to communicate, see if they are relatable or even co-exist with them.

A quirky example of this is the Mel Brooks movie called "Frisco kid."[1] There is a scene in which an Eastern European Jew who emigrated to the USA in the 19th century walks alone in the wild west. In his dazed confusion, he recognizes a group of black robed men on the horizon. He runs toward those persons and shouts "lantzman" (countryman or kin in Yiddish lan-guage), They run toward him as if to help, but don't understand him. The encounter turns to a disappointment when he notices a Christian bible in their pocket. The black robed persons are not Hassidic Jews as he thought, but rather German speaking Christian men wearing similar black garb. He then turns away, thinking to himself that those people will not help him. The point here is that external appearance is used both as a support mech-anism and a segregator.

For outsiders, the external symbolism quickly identifies a threat (real or perceived) without the need to interact or even communicate. It is "easy" to identify an outsider because they look different. The main reason is that "outsiders" need to be quickly identified. It is that group's or individual's first thought of preservation which leads them to believe that an outsider's main purpose of "showing up at your doorstep" is to cause you harm or take your possessions. Quite often that has been the case when wealth accumulation was perpetuated by raiding adjoining tribes or communities. Before any attack there was always information gathering in the form of an outsider coming into a group and observing the members, their rituals and physical layout of their communities. In other words, spies in their midst. Trust and loyalty were devised to protect the group.

We are now ready to further travel along the road in time that leads to segregation and hate.

To recap. We have fear, we have groups, clans, tribes, then we inter-mix gods, deities and their communicators (priests). Add to those rituals, clothing and marking, blend in personal and societal fears and now there is a perfect system to separate one group from another.

I will not get into the morality or immorality of these tribal rituals, but rather point out that they are big contributors to hate in the wrong circles or dictatorial leaderships.

PART II: ROLE OF RELIGIONS IN HATE

CHAPTER 5

Religion, A Controlling Institution

The thinking humans always strived to explain what is happening around them. We needed to understand the how, the why, the when, the who of events, phenomena and behaviors. Unlike animals that accepted their natural surrounding and accepted events as they are, humans needed to rationalize it all. And if they could not explain or rationalize it, humans concluded that there is a greater force or being that is causing it all or manipulating events. This greater force can be in the form of another human, super human (or a god/deity) or forces of nature. Early humans went even further to state that everything in the land is formed by the basic elements of Earth, Wind and Fire. Therefore all humans are subject to these forces, these gods, these deities.

Being mostly fearful and conforming beings, humans allowed the creation of these deities and ceded controls to intermediaries that could communicate with these gods/forces. That group of intermediaries is demonstrated in the form of priests/priestesses, shamans, witch doctors and 'holy men'.

The creation of ritualistic religions ceded powers to intermediaries. The reasoning was that the gods only talked to the ones gifted with a conduit to themselves. Since the gods are all powerful, and sometimes vengeful, we as humans needed to protect ourselves from ill. Essentially, we wanted to appease those forces to not cause us any harm, or ask for help to achieve a goal or a wish. The goals could be as simple as having children (usually males), more property, keep illness, disease or even death away (thoughts and prayers). The next step in appeasing these forces/gods or enlisting their support is the notion that they are on your side and will help you achieve those goals. Did you notice the praying that is going on at schools football fields here in the USA? Does God really cheer for one team over the other? Is this a war of good versus evil that there is a need to pray for victory and strength during a sporting event? If there is a loving god, then there is no point in one side praying for victory over another team.

Once a religion is accepted (by any means), it becomes a dominant force in the community and society. They will dictate rituals, foods you may eat, attire and perform ceremonies such as marriages, coming of age, burials and more. And of course, collect monies (call it donations, mitzvas, tithing, zakat. . . .) Religion comes with a price!

Early institutions based on deities/gods were created both to minimize the wrath of those gods, acts as guides and more importantly intercede to control a population. In many cases symbols of those deities were carried into battles (The Ark of the Covenant, Christian golden crosses during the crusades, Muslim armies fighting in the name of God, etc....). Religious institutions now controlled many aspects of life and even had the powers to select (read anoint) kings and leaders.

Amongst the early Hebrews, the initial concept of a king was rejected by the religious segments. Early prophets did not agree to that notion. However, they realized the value of such a responsibility and thus kings were selected thru them. The ultimate religious selection of a king was King David and his decedents. To further legitimize the new religion, Christianity claims Jesus was genetically connected to King David as delineated in the New Testament Matthews Chapter 1 verse 1 through 16, twenty-eight generations; I wonder how they followed genealogy back then?

Religion not only controlled daily life of the populace, but also was the dominant ingredient in the selection of kings. This was especially prevalent and part and parcel of the Catholic church in Europe. It was a rare occasion when a king was not selected or backed up by the Pope in Rome. The fear of excommunication was a force to be reckoned with and carried practical consequences.

Early on and until the early 20th century, the institution of monarchies was prevalent. However, a king on their own were fearful of losing their power and quickly realized an alliance with a prevalent religion is needed. Thus, holy men, priests and shamans were incorporated into the monarchy. The Jewish bible is replete with stories of those messengers of God advising kings regarding life and going to wars. Soon the position of those advisors became prominent and powerful especially when a weak monarch was manipulated to their wills. Obviously, it was also used by kings in reverse. They excused their actions by stating they are doing god's will. Everyone states that the gods or God are on their side (even the Nazis stated so). The entire affair of the Crusaders was done by European monarchy under the name of a religious duty to liberate the holy land. Even though it was a diversionary tactic away from the troubles in their lands, the population had to comply and go to these made-up religious campaigns. Europeans also justified their pillaging and destruction in the new world as "doing God's work" and convert the "savages" to Christianity. Same in Asia, Australia and other South Pacific regions.

Even today in the 21st century, religion dominate politics and power. Politicians fall over each other to prove they are religious enough by publicly performing acts like going to churches, carrying bibles or starting government/civil meetings with invocations and prayers. The perceived legitimacy given by God allows them to control, limit and in some cases kill those not conforming (we have seen how ISIS followers threw gay men off roof tops in Arab countries because the religious institution they adhere to forbids homosexuality).

CHAPTER 6

The Role of Religion in Hate

The next phase of power preservation is to grow it bigger. Growth however demands planning and resources as well as transforming those resources into deeds. So basically, a leader has a vision, that is then translated into a mission statement. Then there is a need for a master plan going down to a detailed plan. The grander the vision, the more resources are needed. The problem with getting additional resources is that you have to come up with a bigger plan to obtain them. One form of early resource was human power to perform tasks like building or cultivation of food. The progression into the form of servants and slavery emerged. Slavery was well known and documented in early texts. They preceded the early Egyptians and is fully documented through hieroglyphs carved into stone walls and papyrus paper writings. Slavery even is stated openly in the bible. Even Abraham who is considered the "father" of both Judaism and Islam had slaves. No one then had any thoughts that this entire concept of slavery is wrong, even God did not intervene. When Moses came down Mount Sinai with the tablets inscribed with the Ten commandments, there is a mention of keeping the Sabbath holy (no work shall be performed on that day). I just can't help the thought that it was to make sure that the servants do not exhaust themselves working seven days a week. In those days, there was little difference in the treatment of servants or any variation of that.

Reference from the bible book of Exodus: "your male servant, or your female servant"

"Remember the Sabbath day, to keep it holy. Six days you shall labor, and do all your work, but the seventh day is a Sabbath to the LORD your God. On it you shall not do any work, you, or your son, or your daughter, *your male servant, or your female servant,* or your livestock, or the sojourner who is within your gates. For in six days the LORD made heaven and earth, the sea, and all that is in them, and rested on the seventh day. Therefore, the LORD blessed the Sabbath day and made it holy."

There was no thought given to subjugation and slavery other than the purpose of wealth accumulation. Those not part of your society, culture or family were treated as less of a person. The strive for more wealth accumulation and power was garnered via subjugation of humans. Look at slavery in America. A country founded on Christian values treated black slaves from Africa as non-humans requiring subjugations and control. You see, religion is now used as a tool for control. Another graphic example in the 20th century to legitimize control and murder is the creation via "scientific research" of the term "sub human" or as was deemed by some and later in Nazi Germany as "Untermensch." [4]

Wikipedia

The line of reasoning was: "Even though that person sort of looked like me, that person was not developed to the same degree and is to be considered a pollutant that would intermix with my kind and cause having undesirable offspring." That message was routinely used by a conquering power and followed a propaganda message which justified the elimination of that "sub human populace." One would wonder how Neanderthals disappeared?

So where is religion in all of this and why is it used as a tool of hate?

As stated, religion is a further progression in human thinking that we are not masters of ourselves and everything that happens is due to the wishes of a god/deity in a positive way or as a punishment for some transgression done by the individual or society (example is Sodom and Gomorrah destroyed by God). Conformity to a god is a desired if not a required behavior. Life is all good if you behave. Right? Well, that is not what always happens in the mind of humans. Quite often the transgression is self-created or has nothing to do with the individual's or societal control. For example, how is famine considered a transgression by any human in ancient times? How did famine happen? What can a person do to fix famine? One way is to understand that famine happens from time to time and the best way to address it is to store food during the good times and use it during famine. The lack of planning and its negative eventualities has two consequences. The first one is to be honest and admit the lack of preparation and then suffer the deaths and misery that follows and try to remedy the situation. The second form of dealing with disasters is to shirk responsibility and blame it on others. "Bad things are happening to us because those others amongst us caused all the misery experienced," or "their deviant way of life caused this." Or worse yet, "they purposely created this disaster upon us to take over."

Did you notice the QAnon conspiracy theory[1] floated in 2021 and regurgitated by a US congressional member from Georgia as to Jews having lasers in space and they caused the huge wildfires in the Western USA?

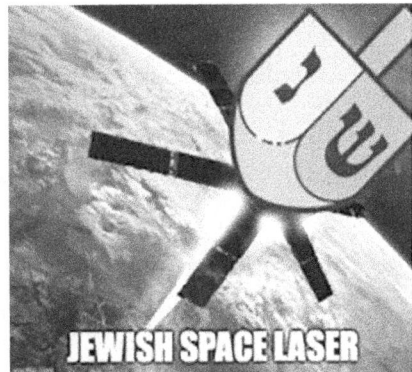

JEWISH SPACE LASER

Or how about Jews are to blame for the COVID-19 pandemic to control the world?[5]

And here is another one in Florida where Disney company is attacked by the Republican governor and his blind minion followers. This packet was found on multiple private home driveways blaming Jews at Disney for being pedophiles.

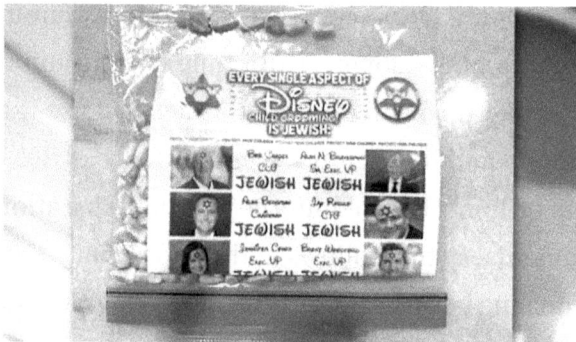

These are just some examples of wholesale blaming Jews for the world and American misery.

All this just discussed is caused by fear! Fear is a basic human trait that is so primal it is difficult to sometimes rationalize. Fear in its basic form is a protector of ourselves. It tells you not to go and pick a fight with a bear or a lion or you will die. It tells you not to enter an unknown cave for there may be an animal that will attack. It also allows the thinking human to look for alternatives short of confrontation (like trade instead of fighting for goods).

On the flip side, fear allows others to manipulate us. Fear was a tool used from early days in its most basic form. "If you don't follow me, you will all die!!!!!." Or if you do not sacrifice you will all suffer! Those "gifted manipulators" used the fear factor to enhance their message and in turn increase their fortunes. Fear in many societies lead to the concepts of Apocalypse, Armageddon, End of time, death and destruction from above, Hell, inferno and eternal suffering.... Those were strong motivators to keep the population in check and use them as needed to consolidate power and wealth.

Now we are ready to discuss the role of religion in all of this.

Religion, worship of deities, paying homage, believing in spirits has multiple rationales and purposes. In its purest form it is the belief that we are incapable of managing our daily life (never mind our life journey). You will hear that everything is pre-ordained, or it is our fate, our destiny and there is nothing we can do other then go on the path chosen for us because we are nothing but pawns of the gods. We are told that we need guidance from above (the gods or God). We are told to receive the guidance, rituals, performances of acts on daily basis. It all requires adherence to rituals like prayers that must be followed. It then manifests itself that believers must conform in order to be considered loyal (or true believers).

It is often repeated that man has transgressed against God/gods and needs to follow a certain regiment to lead a proper life, a just life, and honest life. Without that obedience there cannot be that life and so the concept of sin and sinners was created. In other words, if you do not conform, you are a bad person. "I will call you a sinner, a heretic, apostolic, infidel, a non-believer, or not a true believer."

Here is the main message that can be derived from the Old Testament book of Genesis dealing with the Garden of Eden. "And God said to Adam and Eve, do not eat from the fruit of the apple tree for it surely will kill you." As any curious "child," Eve picked the apple and gave it to Adam to eat. They both did. Wisdom then ensued and they realized they are naked and hid behind fig leaves. What does God do? He punishes the female first in that she will suffer every time she will give birth. However, Adam the male subject here just gets kicked out along with Eve. How wise and just (sarcastic). Sure, punish the female! A vengeful God just had to punish humans knowing full well that he setup the situation in the garden just to have the humans fail.

Religions and deities as stated, were created as soon as humans started expressing their thoughts. The problem that arose is that we are all individuals and therefore have our own interpretation of God. No matter what I have for a god, the next person believes I am wrong and tries to convince me to change (missionaries as an example routinely travel the world telling the locals that they are wrong in their believes and that the correct message is what the missionaries bring). All religions have one thing in common. Their way is always correct, following their ways and rituals removes the fears, improves their way of life and corrects the errors of the "others."

I am reminded of that a poster depicting gods and deities smiling and hugging. The caption is "Humans have 5000 gods and deities, but don't worry only yours is right." [2] Ricky Gervais and Twitter.

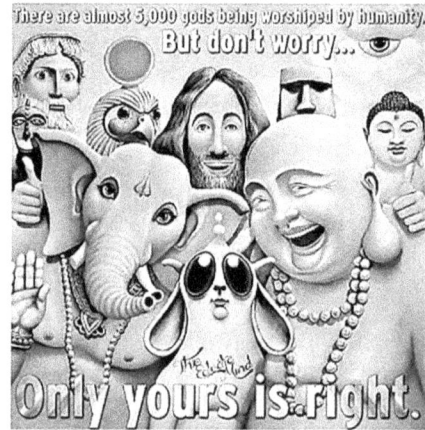

The idea of polytheistic or multiple gods is primal and early form of many religions. To them, events are controlled by multiple gods that sometimes compete among each other and sweep humans up in their quarrels. Greek and Nordic mythology is full of stories of gods quarreling and undermining each other often using humans as pawns. The takeaway here is that you need to please them all or else, you will suffer. It became too much of a task to please them all.

Enter the Monotheistic concept.

The idea here is that there is a single god, an all-mighty God, an ever-present God, an everlasting God. All your needs in the spiritual, psychological, physical and material realms are controlled by a single power. That concept appealed to the early Hebrew founders. It became apparent that something monumental was needed in order to convince the population of this concept. The first step was to leave the place they are in now for a better place. Migrating out, an "exodus," as a large group. This caused immense hardship on the individuals and was devised as a way for "trials and tribulations." A test of sort for those deemed "worthy "of receiving this message of the one God. The early Hebrews as written in the Jewish bible, lived a relative comfortable life. They came from the land of Ur, or Mesopotamia, what is today Iraq.

Here is where a leader says he has a calling from this one God who instructs him (Abram) to destroy all other idols before him. In other words, pick a fight with others that believe in multiple gods by physically attacking those instruments. The rational is that only one god is dominant, and the only one way is to worship this god and all other gods/idols are to be destroyed or ignored. What makes this unique is that there is no attack on the people, but rather an idea. Instead of working on the population to change "convert" to the mono god concept, this leader, Abram (later to become Abraham),[3] picks up the entire family and possession and decides to go on a trek to what is known today as the land of Israel. This trek is under the guidance and direction of God. This God as presented, causes multiple crises and demands obedience. However, whether the obedience is blind, negotiated or confrontational, it is still of the form of doing God's will for a greater purpose.

The mere fact that a religion can now segregate and punish others not part of their camp shows the role it plays in propagating hate and violence in its name. Why destroy my little trinkets of gods? Why call me an Infidel and kill me if I do not convert to Islam? Why pin on me anything that happened thousands of years ago? The simple answer is control. And religion is a perfect tool for subjugation. It is cloaked in mystery and vagueness and provides reasons and excuses for those with ill and evil intent.

CHAPTER 7

Early Christianity and the separation from Judaism

Disciples and followers of Yeshu (the Hebrew name of Jesus) started creating what would be early Christianity. That movement emerged many years after the crucifixion event. None of the texts in the New Testament were written immediately after the event, and most likely the books of the New Testament were written hundreds of years later. This new movement which sprouted out of original Judaism was exported out of the land of Judea and started spreading to nearby lands in what is now Turkey and Greece. The original disciples as described in the New Testament, were Jews from the land of Judea. All were persecuted by the local authorities and felt distant from the prevailing system of governments. They saw the established Jewish authority as a roadblock to their new movement and ideas. Mainly a direct confrontation to biblical beliefs dealing with God, the Messiah and relationship with mankind. One way of dealing with your antagonist is to write a narrative in which your political or religious competitor is vilified as not only to beliefs counter to yours, but also pin the murder of your central figure (Jesus) which according to their beliefs was not only the Messiah, but also the personification of God on earth (the son of God) on the established Jews. Since that narrative was written hundreds of years later, there was no one to dispute or challenge that notion. Further, the entire Mediterranean was part of the Roman empire. As such, if you want to be accepted by the Roman masters or at least minimize persecution, the writers of the New Testament absolved them of anything unsavory or confrontational. Thus, they twisted the event of Jesus crucifixion and pinned it on the Jews they wanted to replace. They created a scenario in which Jews are complicit and the Romans were "just doing the dirty work" of the Jews as is written in Mathew 27:24 that Pontius Pilot (the Roman governor of Judea) who pronounced the death sentence stated "I am innocent of this man's blood," or better stated "I wash my hands" as if to say he had nothing to do with that death sentence and is only carrying the wishes of the Jewish "mob" or the Jewish religious authority, the Sanhedrin. On its face, this is a false narrative since the Romans were in full control of Judea and ruled it mercilessly. Crucifixion was a common form of punishment to anyone challenging their rule. Thousands were crucified before and after Jesus. A direct perceived threat to Roman rule was posed and the Romans decided to kill Jesus. As much as Jesus was portrayed as being confrontational with the Jewish government at that time, Jews were not in a position of controlling themselves and everything done was conforming to the Roman masters. Whomever wrote the New Testament and especially the text of Mathew, had a distinct agenda of attacking the Jewish life at the time, blaming only the Jews with the idea of neutralizing it and ultimately replacing it. The Romans were not a central figure of a new religion; However, they were complicit in influencing or even writing the gospels that way as to shield themselves. Christianity has not only become a new religion, but a fierce replacement to the Jewish thinking and way of life. The written narrative in the New Testament not only pinned the blame of Jesus (a Jewish Rabbi) murder on the prevailing Jewish authorities, but perpetuated a notion that all Jews, no matter how far and wide, present and future are complicit in the murder of Jesus and deserve to be blamed and persecuted and at worse, die (Mathew 27:25 "and all the people answered: his blood be on us and on our children"). This was a sort of insurance to keep Jews away from early Christianity and a political payback of perceived wrong doing at that time. As a student of history, I don't know if the original intent was for initial or immediate results or was it a mechanism to be used in perpetuity. No matter how it was intended, it was a call to action by Christianity to commit Anti-Jewish acts until present day. Some acts were on a grand scale like the Spanish Inquisition of the 1400's, numerous pogroms in Eastern Europe culminating in the Holocaust of World War two. All were perpetuated and justified as Jewish conspiracy against Christians or refusal to convert. The shear fact that the

Catholic church only "absolved" the Jews of the death of Jesus in the 1965 document, Nostra Aetate (the Vatican said the charge of deicide against the Jews was false), and even then, in not a very convincing way. Pope benedict the 16th in 2011 had to reiterate that again in his book about Jesus. This simple fact shows the ingrained and institutionalized anti-Jewish teaching that prevailed and I am sure continues in all sort of Christian denominations. And oh yes, I was told by some "born again Christians" that no true Christian will think that way. And my response was always: really? How do you explain all the Christian lead attacks and persecutions of the Jews? All done in the name of Christianity! Falling into that narrative that True Christians are not that way, allows the rest of the "Christians" to continue Anti-Jewish sentiments and acts. I would encourage those "True believers" to go out and actively correct that misconception.

There was a small problem for this budding new religion in which they saw old Judaism as a threat or competitor to be eliminated. What a better way to succeed then to denigrate your competitors and stating that they are evil no-good doers and that they sinned in the eyes of God. Then write that God has abandoned the Jews and now has a new covenant through Jesus only and everything prior to that is to be eliminated. The narrative changed especially by Romans converted to early Christianity which dissolved any complicity of the ruling Roman powers and shifted the death of the "Son of God," (Jesus who is a Jew) onto the Jews as an entire people. They ignored the fact that they, the Romans controlled the entire region and peoples of their empire (but that detail apparently escaped the story writers) and now created the false narrative that they were simple tools of the Jews. Blame the victims is always a "go-to" in the toolbox of hate. The new Christian narrative by the writers of the New Testament changed to Jesus being considered a "heretic" and a challenger to the Jewish religious leadership in Judea and they only looked to the Romans to execute him. As simple as that narrative is, it carried dire consequences to the entire Jewish population in which all the Jewish people were accused of an inexcusable murder. These writers made the Jews complicit in Jesus's murder and so then they deserved to be punished. But that event happened many years in the past and no one alive at the time the New Testament books were written was connected to that event. But because early Christianity relied on acceptance and conversion from the Roman empire inhabitants, any resistance to their ideas of God and the relationship with their icon/Savior was a threat. Jews, being a people that tended to question things and resist conversion to the point of suicide in the name of God (kidush hashem). They would not convert. The next step was to turn on the Jews by placing collective guilt of the crucifixion event linking it to them.

Another item that should give pause to anyone studying the New Testament, was the fact those texts were written in Greek language.[1] If the disciples were really Jews, most likely they would not have written in that Hellenic language, but rather in their own version of Hebrew (or Aramaic, especially if they wrote religious texts). There were many Jews that were Hellenized and resided outside of Judea at the time. They were already adhering to the Greek thinking and that explains why it was written in Greek. The animosity sewn by the converts laid the groundwork for hate and blame writing. That brings me to the facts that the Greeks at the time are constantly described in the Old Testament (the Jewish bible) as attacking the Hebrews and constantly trying to convert them. The famous story of the Maccabees[2] illustrates that vividly in which a Hebrews were fighting back to reassert Jewish rule back in their homeland.

Now the ground work for Anti-Jewish sentiments, attacks, murders and ultimately mass murders has been laid out as early as the first, second and third centuries. It became easy for this sentiment to propagate primarily because most of the early and even later Christian converts were not from the land of Judea nor were Jewish. If the early missionaries were out there spreading their religion were to succeed, they separated the Jews from the rest of the world population and then propagate the narrative of hate toward the Jews. People far and wide in Europe and Asia who never even heard of Jews or even knew where Judea was, suddenly are armed with false knowledge and continued the same false narrative of holding all Jews responsible of Jesus crucifixion and therefore are worthy of attacks and destruction.

CHAPTER 8

Islamic World and Jews
Early Times and Today

Islam as a religion came upon about 500 years after Christianity was formed. Its origin is traced to what is now Saudi Arabia. It draws upon information from both Judaism and Christianity and forms itself as the only true message of God (a quick observation: every religion claims the same). In its effort to convert others to its brand, it painted Jews as faulty and the reason that God abandoned them in favor of Islam. Islam is a proselytizing religion and is known for its approach with the sword in that mission. The stage is already set for conflict.[1] When the Arabs finally took over Judea, the Jews were neither in any power nor position to resist. And those that did resist or refused to convert were in many instances murdered (The Arabic saying of "Itbah al Yahud,"[2] literally means Slaughter the Jews). Jews that did not convert were at most tolerated (as long as they paid protection tax). Jews were marginalized yet again in their own homeland. However, the conquest by the Arab Muslims of the land known to the Jews as Judea or Palestine to the Greeks, Romans and Christians, created a new scenario for conflict. The conditions on the ground became more of a conflict between European Christians and Muslim that manifested itself in hundreds of years of Crusades and "Holy wars." Jews were just collateral damage between the two conflicting religions.

Once the Christian Crusaders finally realized that they can no longer control Judea/Israel/Palestine, the Muslim powers dominated the entire Middle East region. As Islamic power was consolidated, Jews became second class inhabitants and became a target for conversion. Islam has a "soft clause" in that you will not be converted by force, only by free will.

However, if your life is constantly harassed or marginalized or is threatened by other means, sooner or later many would convert. Those that would not convert were then forced to have identifying marks on their clothing and pay "protection" fee. And to show that the Jews were paying this fee, they were forced to wear identification marking. In addition, Jews were made to defer to the Muslim population with what appears to be completely stupid and idiotic deference. A Jew had to move aside when a Muslim was walking toward him/her. "Wicked or evil Jews" were painted as dirty animals, dogs, pigs. . . . That and other practices of denigration were used again and again. (Nazis used the same tactics).

A little more detail:

Now fast forward to the 20th century in which many people are aware of the Jewish star that was forced upon by the Nazis and their enablers.

Jewish badge worn during the Holocaust and prior [3]

Most people recognize this version of a symbol identifying Jews during the Holocaust, but this was only the latest practice of visually branding Jews from the local dominant population.

In Muslim controlled countries, the wearing of special marking by non-Muslims (Dhimmis) was introduced early on. It was introduced in the Umayyad Caliphate by Caliph Umar II in the early 8th century. The practice continued and reinforced by Caliph Al-Mutawakkil (847–861) and remained enforced for centuries after. A Genizah document from 1121 gives the following description of decrees issued in Baghdad (a Genizah is a storage area in a Jewish synagogue or cemetery designated for the temporary storage of worn-out Hebrew-language books and papers on religious topics prior to proper cemetery burial):

"Two yellow badges are to be displayed, one on the headgear and one on the neck. Furthermore, each Jew must hang round his neck a piece of lead with the word Dhimmi on it. He also has to wear a belt round his waist. The women have to wear one red and one black shoe and have a small bell on their necks or shoes." Now Jews were treated like cattle amidst the Muslim communities with bells for all to hear them coming and stay away from.

The primary objective of these identifiers was to easily separate non-Muslims (in this case Jews) from the majority Muslim population. This was done as a show of both dominance and the collection of special "protection" fee (Jizyah) that was exacted on the "non-believers" (the Muslim way of identifying those that would not convert to Islam).[4]

More details as to the treatment of Jews and Christians under Islam is better illustrated in this book.[5]

The Dhimmi: Jews and Christians Under Islam.
Bat Ye'or author, 1985 available on Amazon.

Modern Islam directed anti-Jewish doctrine and treatment; Israel is reestablished in 1948.

There were numerous Anti-Jewish incidents in Muslim controlled regions prior and during the early 20th century, however, those incidents increased dramatically as a result of the war of independence for the state of Israel in 1948. That conflict between Arabs and Jews in Palestine/Israel, created a major population shift in the region which further contributed to the rift between those two people. It is understandable that rift between the two conflicting parties would have escalated and ultimately come to a war. Jews finally had an official homeland to return to, but the Arab population that fled to surrounding Arab countries were not welcomed there amongst their own brothers. Instead of integration, they were forced into refugee camps until today. There was no attempt to absorb them into those Arab societies even though they were related or even the same prior to the British/French partition of the entire Middle East after World War One. Instead, those refugees are used as a tool to perpetuate the hate and the desired outcome; the destruction of Israel ("push the Jews to the sea"). This single aspect of Arab refugees is unique in which no other conflict resulted in permanent refugee status. That even includes wars between India and Pakistan. Both sides separated from greater India. There are no refugee camps in either country. Even at the conclusion of hostilities in Europe after World War Two, with millions of refugees, camps existed for a short time and all were resettled around the world within a few years. There are no refugee camps remaining from that monumental conflict.

The rift between Muslims and Jews extended far and wide into the Arab and Islamic world. Muslims in faraway countries committed Anti-Jewish acts and in essence exacerbated the population shifts. In 1948 war of Independence, Arabs residing in Israel (known as Palestine prior to 1948) left or were forced out due to fear mongering circulated that the Jews will massacre them. Jews in Arab countries were fiercely persecuted and forced out of Arab and Muslim controlled lands. Many emigrated to Israel during the 1950's. By the 1970's the Jewish population in Muslim countries was practically zero.

Why is it that Muslims in Pakistan, Iran, Indonesia etc. would get involved and proceed to alienate themselves from Jews and Israel in particular? Most Muslims in those countries never even saw a Jew (since none reside there nor is welcomed). I would venture to say that most Muslims do not know why they personally hate Jews.

The simple answer is that this hate is perpetuated directly by the political religious leaders that constantly bring back the narrative that Jews wronged God, and God is punishing them (using Muslims as a tool to exact that punishment). This phenomenon has been exacerbated after Israel became independent state.

The denigration of minorities has been a tried-and-true tool of monolithic societies especially when dictatorship like control is practiced. In a

Muslim world, there is no separation of religion from the state. They are the same. The religious leaders have described themselves as getting their input from their Quran which is the "words of God." Their interpretation is unquestionable and the populace just follows.

By the 1980s, according to historian Bernard Lewis, the volume of antisemitic literature published in the Arab world seemed to suggest that classical antisemitism had become an essential part of Arab intellectual life. The rise of political Islam during the 1980s and afterwards provided a new variant of Islamic antisemitism.

Enter Iran

Here is where things really get convoluted. Iran has been ruled by a person installed by the United States CIA in 1954 in a coup. The purpose of that coup was a means of controlling the oil in the Middle East after World War Two. That person was crowned a Shah or Emperor with no legitimacy. The Shah exerted control over the populace and was harsh on the local Muslim Shia clergy. As events rolled out, the Shah was deposed from power in 1979 by a revolution lead and inspired by a Muslim cleric Ayatollah Khomeini who became a Supreme leader. This is where the new religious controlled government turned their attention to the USA and Israel. Now it is understandable why they considered the USA as their enemy (the USA created and supported the repressive regime of the Shah), but at the same time, that venom was directed toward Israel and Zionism.

How is it that Israel and Jews got on the "bad" side of Iranian Islamist government?

Israel role in Iran during the Shah's reign

Israel early on, was looking for allies and support in the Middle east and provided some support to the Iranian regime of the Shah. That included both military advice and commercial projects. That aspect is no different than any country that wants good relations and economic trade. It was not overt nor covert, since the USA was the dominant supplier of military and commercial projects. However, once the Iranian Islamic revolution was entrenched, this relationship changed and somehow Israel became the "boogie man" to the Iranian regime. Again, the reason is easy to understand. If you want to make changes and force people to your cause, you find a scape goat (the Jews), harp on them as if they are the cause of your misery and constantly harass them. That hate was draped in Anti-Israel and Anti-Zionist flavor instead of outright Anti-Jewish. The verbiage had the same results. Constant verbal attacks against Israel were backed up physically by the proliferation of military hardware to militant proxies created in the Middle East (like Hezbollah in Lebanon) that regularly attacked Israel via acts of terror and missile attacks.

There is a little side note in the post Iranian revolution and Israeli relation that is perplexing. During the Iran-Iraq war of the 1980's, Israel quietly supplied military spare parts to Iran (primarily aircraft parts for F-4 Phantom jets Iran originally purchased from the USA). Since Iraq was a sworn enemy of Israel (It started during the 1948 war of Israeli independence and continues to this day), Israel's governments took to the misguided notion of "the enemy of my enemy is my friend" and secretly provided the parts while publicly being bashed by the Iranian regime. That calculation by Israel was faulty and short sighted. It did not provide any benefit or good will and instead painted Israel as an opportunistic devil.

As time progressed and economic conditions in Iran deteriorated after the prolonged bloodletting war with Iraq, Iranian leadership sharpened their rhetoric. It then embarked on another tried and true tool and that is to separate the Jews from Israel or Zionism. They went on to say that they are against the "Zionist entity." Israel should be wiped off the face of the earth." "Iran is not against Jews, but against Israel." They went as far as having conferences in Iran in 2006 on the topic of the Holocaust and invited fringe Ultra-Orthodox Jews that are themselves against the state of Israel (Neturei Karta). Those are Jews that believe the Messiah (and Jesus is not the Jewish Messiah) still has not showed up to free the Jews, so Israel as a Jewish land cannot be formed and Israel as a country should not exist.

Neturei Karta during Al Quds day in Germany. from Common Wiki

Not that the Iranian clergy needs Jewish support, but it does welcome this fringe narratives that contributes to further Anti-Semitism by those Jews themselves. By inviting an opposing group of Jews with their own interpretation of biblical writing, the process chips away Jewish legitimacy.

Zionism painted as an oppressor

The new phenomenon of Anti-Jewish, Anti-Israel sentiments has shifted away from strictly Anti-Semitic rhetoric and into Zionism (a Jewish movement advocating homeland in Israel). Basically, that narrative is trying to convince liberal minds that Israel is a white colonial power that segregates and separate the Jews from Arabs especially in the West bank. By keeping it as a colonial power and a subjugated people, the entire narrative takes on a simple human rights issue and nothing more. Israel is viewed as an Apartheid state (after the South African White only rule system). Even Nelson Mandela, a symbol of institutional racism victim in the modern times came against Israel as such. Instead of engaging Israel's government directly and offering a solution to the Arab Israeli conflict, it is scientifically expedient to just paint Israel as an "entity," a "colonial power," a "subjugator" and worst as an "ethnic cleansing regime." It even goes further to the realm that Jews were never in the land they called Palestine. And as if that is not enough to delegitimize Jews, there is also the narrative that European Jews are really not Jews at all, but converts of Central Asia called Khazers. The tactics of delegitimizing works well especially in coordinated and persistent attacks. Modern socially conscience people (especially on the liberal spectrum) do not want to understand the Jewish plight as they join Anti-Israel movements. Instead of working toward a common cause of peaceful existence, they attack and provoke the situation further away. I venture to say, that at the end, they too will be the victims of their own chants.

Finally, effort to dismantle Israel by attacking the political movement of Zionism which was instrumental in the creation of the state of Israel and a safe haven for Jews will persist. Regardless of internal Israeli politics or the interaction with Arabs, one cannot summarily dismiss Jews living in Israel. Unfortunately, religion is the one major obstacle for quiet cohabitation of the land by those that have historical ancestral claim or the Arab inhabitant living there for hundreds of years. There is enough land to share and live in peace. True peace will never happen because hate is so engrained in humans that it makes it difficult to coexist.

PART III: WHO ARE THE JEWS?

CHAPTER 9

Biblical Judaism and Jews

Let's go back to the beginning of Judaism.

The Bible in the book of Genesis describes individuals residing in what is today's Iraq's fertile lands between the two big rivers of Euphrates and Tigris. It goes further to describe a person in the name of Abram who encounters God and is given the task to shed the prevalent idol gods. The second task is to pick up and depart toward the west into the land of Canaan (today's Israel). Abram manages to convince his family and brother Lot, to pick up and follow him. The group follows voluntarily to a faraway land and creates an integrated society based on agriculture and herding livestock. Abram then has a covenant with God and a new religion is formed, the Hebrews. After time passes, the Hebrews want a king as in other cultures. Initially, this notion is rejected, but a king is finally selected (anointed) and a dynasty is created. The king that is finally accepted as the king of the Hebrews is King David. He is selected as a rival to King Saul after Saul commits suicide by falling on his sword. King David is now the ruler over the Hebrews and according to the bible, is selected by God to rule. King David's dynasty is not long lived and after his son's rule, King Solomon, the Hebrews like other humans begin to fight amongst themselves and slowly disintegrates culminating in disastrous conquests from outside (Babylonians, Assyrians, Greeks, Romans . . .)

Like any form of religion or a way of life, a leader is selected and anointed. The leader becomes a king or absolute ruler of a people. Once that is established, kings and rulers create conflicts with other kings and wars start in which the loser and their people are subjugated to the wills of the winning side. As we go through reading the Old Testament, it is replete with acts of wars and conquests. Early on, the victories of the Hebrew Kings are described, but then the story of loss of faith, vanquish, deportation and subjugation as God's punishments is written.

The first mass deportation of Jews (Hebrews) by force is by the Babylonian conqueror king Nebuchadnezzar. Jews were forced to leave the land of Israel and Judea and march on to the east and away (book of Daniel 1:1). This type of collective punishment may have started as a way of diluting the opposition to the rulers, but quickly turned into a creation of fear to keep a minority population in check. Stories of defiance and resistance (passive mostly) are told as in Daniel in the lion's den and that of Ester (King Ahasuerus of Persia selected a Jewish woman by the name of Ester (whose actual name was Hadassah) in saving her people from the king's wrath.

The second major deportation occurred by the Romans in which after Jewish resistance and rebellion, the Romans resorted to the sacking of the seat of culture and religion of the subjugated Hebrews to slavery and ousting many from their land in Judea. That symbol of Judaism was the temple in Jerusalem. There was a concerted effort by the Romans to eliminate everything that the Jews stood for, then deport the majority of the population to Roman held territories and the city of Rome. Jerusalem was sacked, destroyed and pillaged to eliminate Jewish resistance.

A further elimination of Jewish resistance was the siege and ultimate

Roman pillage of Jerusalem as carved on the Arch of Titus in Rome (Wikipedia Common)

mass suicide of the cornered Jews on the mountaintop of Masada. Hebrew: מצדה, meaning "fortress"

In addition to Jewish resistance to Rome, there was also a passive resistance in the form of ideology. Multiple personalities emerged of which one in particular created a thorn in the side of the Romans as depicted in the New Testament. That person was known as Yeshu in Hebrew or Jesus in Greek/Latin and English languages. The

Mesada. Wikipedia Common

Romans did not tolerate a resistance or a refute of the rules and created a situation in which the resident Jewish religious organization known as the Sanhedrin was implicated in the killing by crucifying Yeshu as a form of fear and intimidation to the local population. The situation would have been no different than any other Roman crucifixion done at any of their conquered territories before and after Jesus (rebellion and crucifixion of Spartacus comes to mind).

A sidenote

As part of my research for this book, I looked into early Christianity and tried to understand who wrote those books/gospels/New testaments. It is agreed that those books were not written at the time of Jesus, but rather many hundreds of years later. Whomever wrote those texts, their motivation is subject to interpretations. One outlier hypothesis that caught my attention is that it was the Romans that actually wrote or influenced those narratives. They depict actual events perpetrated by themselves, but interjected a mystical person (Jesus) into the mix in order to deflect their responsibility as a further means of Jewish persecution.

The practice of story characters substitution is known to have taken place at the time as evident in biblical stories like the great flood and Noah's ark. This was common in Babylonian and Middle Eastern cultures. It is entirely plausible that the Romans performed the same deed, however, the purpose was not just to regurgitate a story (like the Ark), but rather shift responsibility and create a new narrative.

CHAPTER 10

Who is a Jew?

Before delving into the study of hate as it pertains to Anti-Semitism and Anti-Jewish acts, there is a need to identify a fundamental question:

"Who is a Jew"?

This one question is quite explosive on its own. Even before exposing opposition to Jews (in any and all forms) by non-Jews, it has served to separate Jews amongst Jews themselves.

However, the true definition to an Anti-Semite as to Who is a Jew is immaterial as they are opposed to anything and everything that is attributed to Jews even if they are not Jews at all.

Here we go:

The English language terms of Jew, Jewish, Hebrew, Israelite, Judean, Israeli and many other variations in other languages refers to a people, a culture, a religion, a way of life. In reality, the definition is not straight forward.[5]

On the Jewish religious side, there are multiple interpretations, practices, texts, laws just like in any other religion. You have the orthodox Jews, Chasidic Jews (Ultra-Orthodox, also known as Haredim), Conservative Jews, Reform Jews, Humanistic Jews and even secular or non-practicing, non-religious people. There are even those born having some Jewish roots or identify themselves as Jews.

Some view it as different shades of the same religion, while others see it as different interpretations of texts and rituals and a way of life, while others just participate in knowing they are part of the Jewish identity. The internal rift of who is a Jew is also front and center to the ultra-orthodox which have dominated that definition and Jewish life. This is especially prominent in the state of Israel since its independence in 1948.

Replacement "Jews" are not considered to be Jews

There are groups of people that claim to be the "true Israelites" whose aims are political and do not identify themselves as part of the Jewish collective, but rather want to expel everyone else's definition of who is a Jew (Black Hebrews Israelites).

On the Christian side I heard that they are "Perfected Jews" as in Anne Coulter a right-wing provocateur interview in 2007 on CNBC.[7]

Ethnic Jews

On the ethnic side, the first Hebrews or Jews that inhabited the land of Israel were broken down into 12 tribes. Right away, you are starting with divisions and differences even though genetically and culturally they were all the same people. That division further split the early Hebrews into two. Israel and Judea, each ruled under a separate king, but sharing the same religion. That further weakened them and made it easy for external conquerors to take over. Since the Romans forced many Jews away from Judea 2000 years ago, Jews have lived in many parts of the world far and wide. In some areas like Ethiopia and Somalia, there were Jews that trace their roots to biblical times (decedents of the Queen of Sheba). This makes geographical sense since people traveled along from Egypt to Ethiopia up the Nile River. Other migration of Jews occurred during the many Muslim military conquests in Asia, North Africa and areas under Turkish Ottoman controlled European lands.

What does a Jewish person look like then? It's complicated! Jews are white, black, Middle Eastern, from the Arab peninsula, Latino, Eastern European, Western European, North African, South African, South Americans, from India, American, Australians, Asian. . . . That means, looking at a person, you will be hard pressed to tell that you are looking at what some characterize as a Jewish person.

Rituals and holidays of Jewish people

Do you think that you can spot a Jewish person by the rituals they perform? That is partially true, however it depends on where that Jewish person came from as well as what version of Jewish practice is being utilized (many do not observe).

Many Jewish people that consider themselves religious do practice the observance of the Shabbat (Sabbath). Also, holidays like Rosh Hashana (beginning of the Jewish year), Yom Kippur (day of atonement), Pesach (Passover or commemoration of the exodus from Egypt), Hanukah (the commemoration of the struggles against the Greeks occupiers of their land and more.

Clothing and appearances

Since Jews come from many locations around the world, their clothing[1] reflects the uniqueness of their places. In addition, the belonging to a particular religious or being secular also influences their outside appearances. Some see Chassidic Jews are a representative of all Jews. You see black robes/long coats, white shirts and especially the big hats (sometimes lined with furs). These clothing and hats are relatively new and are unique to Eastern European Jews that formed their own interpretation of Judaism and elected to have unique and identifying clothing and head gear

Common Wiki pics

to differentiate themselves from others. Most European Anti-Semitic acts, propaganda, cartoons tend to use that as a depiction of Jews.

Jews from North Africa and the Middle East and as far as India wore clothing that are more resembling with their local inhabitants. Depending on locations and communities, Jews were made to wear badges and markings on their clothing to identify them as Jews. So as a prelude to the Nazi Holocaust, Jews often were forced to wear an identifier like the Star of David on their clothing. This was prevalent not only in Christian societies, but also lands controlled by Muslims (see the chapter regarding Islam and Jews).

Wikimedia Common

Circumcision

Another way that Male Jews have been identified was presence of male's penis circumcision. This is a ritual performed on a Jewish male where the foreskin of an 8-day old male child is cut in a religious act. It is described in the Jewish Bible book of Genesis as a symbolism of a covenant with God. Abraham performed this circumcision on himself, if you can believe it! If there was a doubt by the perpetrators of Anti-Semitism, the separation of male Jews from non-Jews, it was using circumcision as the segregator. As much as that is mostly true about Jewish males, there are differences here as well. First, Jews are not the only ones that circumcise their males. Muslims do it as well (although that ritual is performed at a later time (usually at age of seven, but can be done earlier or later). Also, depending on countries of residence, circumcision is done as an elective procedure in hospitals on non-Jewish male babies.

The takeaway here is that Circumcision is often used to identify Jewish males, but that does not always identify that person as Jewish.

Lineage

Religious Jews tend to identify themselves as such if the mother of the child is Jewish. This was done primarily as an absolute confirmation that the mother carries the child to term and birth's the baby which is then witnessed by the family and local community. It is relatively easy to confirm who the mother of the child is. As far as the father, it is often difficult and especially early on when the men traveled for work, or were not at home for long stretches of time. The concern was that you may not know for sure who the father of the child was, or if he was Jewish at all.

How do orthodox Jews consider if you are a Jew or not?

—If the mother and father are both Jewish, does it make you Jewish? Yes!

—If the mother is Jewish, and the father is not or unknown, is the child Jewish? Yes! But not if the child is brought up in a Christian or Muslim environment, where paternity is dominant and the mother is just a vessel for carrying the child. That however has been a discovery for some children born to Jewish parents, but because of wars, they were given away by their Jewish parents to be safe (by Christians). Then it is up to the grown-up child to decide to stay Christian or identify themselves as Jews (Madeline Albright comes to mind).

—If the father is Jewish and the mother is not, is the child then Jewish? That answer is mostly no according to orthodox interpretation. Unless the mother converts to Judaism, the child is not considered Jewish. That interpretation is disputed on a personal level and depends on the community one lives in. To some in less than orthodox communities it makes no difference to the individual and they feel Jewish regardless of the orthodox interpretation.

The conflict of who is a Jew is continuing, and many non-orthodox Jews are completely bypassing those barriers. They are forcing the legislative and Judiciary in Israel to consider non-orthodox interpretation (in regards to marriage, having children and even refusing to circumcise their males).

Now it goes further into the NO territory as parents and grandparents lose their identification of being Jewish. Since Jews do not proselytize, and in reality, make it extremely difficult to convert to Judaism, the pool of Jewish people is mostly organically grown and does not rely on external addition to the ranks. The further away from orthodoxy, the looser is the definition.

A secretive and often ignored segment of Jews are the Spanish and Portuguese, Marranos and Conversos.[4]

Those were Jews during the Spanish inquisition in the 1400's, were force converted to Christianity (Catholicism), but secretly continued to practice some Jewish rituals. Over the centuries, those rituals bear little resemblance to Jewish ones. Those individuals and families felt it was important to continue their identities while externally displaying Christianity. This resilience and self-preservation can be attributed to their Jewish identity over the hundreds and thousands of years before the Inquisition.

As an aside, Jews living in Spain and Portugal voluntarily migrated there with the Islamic Caliphate expanding into northern Africa and ultimately to Spain via the Straights of Gibraltar. Since Jews were mostly tradesman, craftsman, handled money, their talents were in demand and they traveled with the Muslim caliphate both to the west as well as to the east (some say there are millions of "Jews" in China).

Reform Jews have been around since the 1800's in Germany and Britain. They have been a counter to the more zealot version of Jews such as the Ultra-orthodox (Hassidic) or Jews of Eastern Europe which formed at the same time.

Reform Judaism was brought to the USA and continued its evolution and changes.

And then, there are the Humanistic Jews that are much more open to interpretation of being Jewish and are more welcoming of interpretations of who is a Jew. That movement is also nonjudgmental of those who are not Jewish, but identify with the Jewish Humanistic aspect.

Who is a Jew? Nazi definition

During Nazi Germany rise to power in the 1930's and the planned extermination of Jews, the definition of who is a Jew was front and center to their doctrine. The main objective of the Nazis, was to pin German, European and world troubles on the Jews. To them this was an expedient tool to tap into European Anti-Semitism which was prevalent, and build upon it as a force unifier to Germans in particular and also to later conquered countries. To the Nazis it was a matter of efficiency and practicality. It really did not matter to them who or what or why, it became a rallying cry to their consolidation of power. To them the definition of who is a Jew became loose. If you had Jewish blood from even one grandparent, then you were considered Jewish and that person was subject to deportation and extermination. Even those Jews that converted to Christianity were persecuted and killed.

Here is a Nazi chart as to who is considered a Jew:

Basically, the Nazis dispensed with the question and just needed a target. The target were the Jews! However, in true Scientific justification, they came up with bogus rules and charts known as the Nuremberg law.[8]

Political divisions in American politics on the question of Who is a Jew

This question of who is a Jew has been circulating for years and centuries. It is especially active question around the more Orthodox Jews and is designed to separate, deprive and control one Jew over another. This is true when it comes to marriage, birth and other rights and privileges. However, lately I noticed that being Jewish and participating in the political process has entered the realm of defining who is a Jew. On the left side of politics, I see calls for Jews not to vote for a Republican and if you do, you are not a Jew. On the right side of American politics, there is another narrative that American Jews voting for Democrats are really not Jews. I noticed in the past few years a young Jewish Right-wing politically conservative commentator[6] is trying to separate Jews into factions (and basically dismissing them as non-Jews or bad Jews as though he has the right and powers of that declaration).

The simple fact of Jews immersing themselves into politics is not unique and shows they care about the political process and human rights. But internal separation by Jews from other Jews for political gain just provides further ammunition to Jewish haters to verbally attack Jews as a matter of course.

To be fair though, I saw a similar treatment in which Christian organizations and their leaders came up with statements that "you are not a Christian if you vote democrat." Or how about the slogans of: "Catholics for Trump"

and not to be outdone, "Jews for Trump"?

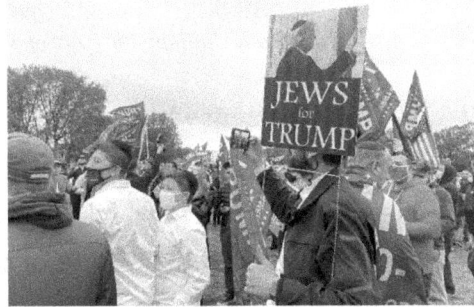

Religion and politics intersection is just headed into more confrontation and violence. Sounds familiar? It should be. European Catholic and Protestant Christians battled amongst themselves for centuries and it continues till today in places like Northern Ireland.

Non-Jews separating Jews to fit their own narratives

For many years, I came across another Anti-Semitic (in disguise) line in American politics. That is to tie the Jewish Holocaust survivor and billionaire philanthropist George Soros[3] and other liberal Jews like the Rothschilds to everything anti American and prove that Jewish money controls the American as well as world politics. Instead of dealing with where he stands as a person, there is a higher importance to them to connect him with being a Jew.

Another approach in political Anti-Semitism is the notion of replacement of Jews. Here is an example in which that exact approach is used by a Right-wing political personality. To paraphrase, "I am more Jewish than that Jew"!!!!!! In other words, a non-Jew (Catholic) is interjecting a Jewish definition onto a Jew for the purpose of denigrating and attacking a person supporting causes not aligned with Right Wing politics:

Rudy Giuliani: I'm more of a Jew than George Soros[2]

It is a losing argument when someone parrots' stupid statement about "real Jews," "real Christian," "real Patriot," "real Republican" (versus RINO). It is all nonsense trash talk in which the purveyors of those statements want to elevate themselves or their cause for the purpose of not only shaming their targets, but to isolate them as though they are some sort of a space alien from another planet that does not belong here on earth. It is all another form of hate!!

Why the fascination of Jews and their "stranglehold on world finances"?

I hear it again and again. "Jews control the world of banking, Jews manipulate politics through money, Jews pervert our values, Jews have space lasers that start wildfires in the western USA...."

Of interest to me is why make the connection of a rich person that has political, ethical, moral views and financially supports causes to being a Jew? Why is it so important to push that narrative in that way? Is there a similar treatment of other rich people when they support their causes? Is anyone emphasizing the religion of other rich people and their causes and financial support? Does anyone out there say "Oh, that Bill Gates the *Christian* is supporting causes that I do not like"? How about other philanthropists? Dare anyone say the Rockefellers, Fords, etc.... as Christian manipulators?

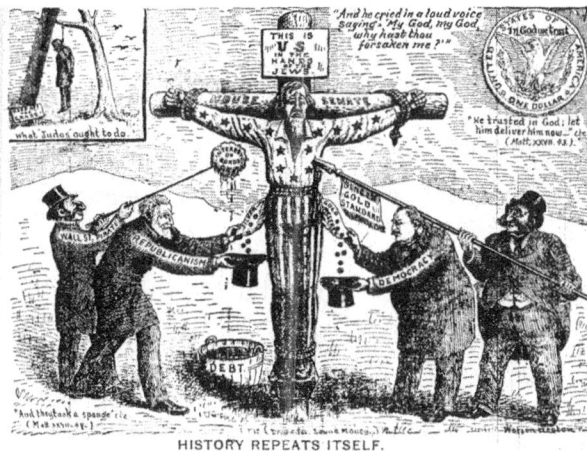

HISTORY REPEATS ITSELF.

"Uncle Sam is crucified and bled by Jews propaganda"

A Jewish banker sits on a sack of gold controlling the stock market

The simple answer is that Anti-Semitism/Anti-Jewishness is engrained in the upbringing of a person growing up in some Christian and Muslim homes. People hear it from grandpa, grandma, mom, dad, uncles.... and just parrot that narrative blindly (Jews killed Jesus, Jews pervert our morality, Jews want to replace us and Jews must die collectively). There is no thought to it. It is received as pure absolute truth and that is all. There is no attempt to describe an individual person doing good or bad without interjecting that they are Jewish. If Anti Semites do not like a Jewish person or their looks, or their philanthropy, politics or mannerism etc. they revert to an easy narrative that this person is evil, he represents everything bad, he is a menace to me and my community, he killed my savior (Jesus) and I will do what I can to discredit him not as an individual or even a human being, but bring in the aspect of that person being Jewish. That kind of rhetoric's just implicated all the Jews in their plot to discredit that one person (target). Why is it important for anyone to devolve into this self-righteousness of separating Jews for the purpose of incriminating all? Why is it important to invoke the "target" person's religion? This kind of behavior also extends to conservative minded Jewish philanthropists like the Koch brothers which are routinely vilified by the Left leaning individuals. So there really is no difference if a conservative or a Liberal uses that tactic of religious separation and vilification. Jews fall into both right and left of politics. No different than any other ethnic or religious group.

Why do it?

It falls into the prime objective of collective blame and is a prime venue into the old method of "divide and conquer." It is one of the oldest most successful methods of subjugation. If you want your deeds done in a diverse place, just pin one side against another. Support one side and vilify the other. It is not only used to separate people based on religion, but also culture, gender, looks, mannerism, tribes, haves vs. have nots (rich vs. poor) or sexual orientation.

The takeaway here is that the question of "Who is a Jew" carries with it both internal and external divisiveness. Both lead to persecution and violence against Jews.

PART IV: ANTI-SEMITISM

CHAPTER 11

The Age of Enlightenment and Race Science Movement

The Age of Enlightenment in Europe during the 17th and 18th century,[1] and its progression further through the 19th century was a time of questioning. Nature and existing Christian dogmas and morality, rejecting monarchies "anointed by God" and promoting individuality were topics to explore. These were good topics to overthrow the yoke of blind obedience to the established rulers. Intellectuals used the sciences and reasoning to explain human nature and the cosmos around them. That in turn had opened up deep questions, but also had unintended outcome when looking for facts that will suit the beliefs and biases of the religious researchers and their benefactors. As science became a big influencer, ideas of humanity and anthropology became a center of attention. Specifically, some were deep in study to explain the difference in human races, cultures, evolution, physical and mental makeup. Darwin explained his theory of evolution of animals and humans. However, some took it further through the use of scientific tools to "explain" the differences between Jews, Christians and others in Europe. The irrational notion of fear perpetuated through dogmas and religious teachings entered the "rational" world by legitimizing Anti-Semitism as a simple fact of nature. From there, it was an easy Segway to characterize Jews as primitive and animal like and thus are the "source of evil"; a direct threat to the Christian world. Scholars in the late 18th, 19th and mid-20th centuries wrote extensively on this subject, and it became a basis of race studies that ultimately paved the way to the next major horrific mass attack on Jews in Europe. That being the Holocaust perpetrated by Nazi Germany.

Since the early times and through the Middle Ages and including the 17th century, explanations of nature, cosmos and events were the realm of religion, superstitions and stark beliefs. This became an end for those seeking scientific proof. You either believed what they taught you at home or in church, or not (at your peril). As science grew religion was not eliminated nor sidelined, but rather took a new approach by selectively embracing science. However, what could be used to support biblical narratives was kept and others not compatible with the whims of the church, were discarded. An earlier example is Copernicus (in the 1500's) finding that the earth and our planets in our solar system rotated about the sun and not the earth, or that the earth was a sphere and not flat. That did not go well with the Catholic Church at the time. Control of the sciences became ever more important to the church. Scientists where not at all atheist. Many were still conforming and some created scientific narratives that matched religious teachings. One such narrative (deniers and all), pinned the ills on the bad genetics of Jews. Thus, the sciences of Eugenics[2] in the 19th and into the 20th century created a "study" that the human species had faulty traits that needed to be eliminated and then improved by "pruning" (really killing) and selective breeding (like pruning trees). This led to a push for an "improved" human race through the intervention of governments. The outcome of this movement was the discrimination of people considered inferior that lead to killing and genocide of those belonging to an "undesirable race" (like the Jews). Amazingly, the American Eugenic society continued until the 1940's. Nazi Germany took a lot of their material and integrated it into their "master race" theory and ultimate genocide of the Jews (and other so called "inferior" people) during the Holocaust.

Like anything else in time and history, something good such as questioning what's around you and what's controlling you can also be used as a tool for separation and segregation. This chapter points out the continuing evolution of questioning and how science can be used to subvert and separate.

If I may extend the enlightenment topic a bit into today's age, look at the Internet as the modern-day equivalent of that period. A vast medium of good that questions everything, provides wonderful information backed by reality and good research, can also be subverted into spreading divisive and hateful messages wrapped up in junk science and bogus material to support it.

Eugenics posters and "studies"

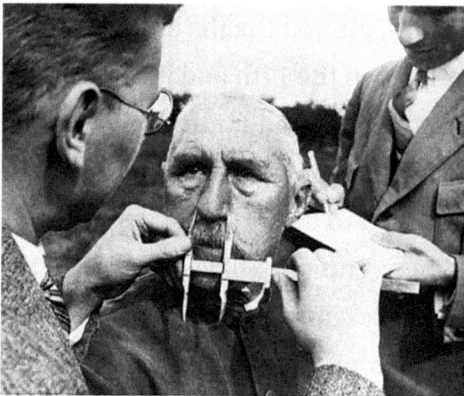

Measurements of facial features to classify humans.

A Nazi chart depicting a "deviant" population will grow to if allowed to reproduce.

Berlin.- Exhibition "Wonders of Life." Exhibition board with graphics and text "That's how it would end. Qualitative population increase with insufficient reproduction of the higher-ranking / According to Burgdörfer 'people without youth'. / This is how it will happen when the lower-ranking have 4 children and the higher-ranking have 2 children."

Bundesarchiv Bild 102-16748, exhibition 'Wonder of Life' rotate crop. jpg (Wikimedia)

CHAPTER 12

Anti-Semitism, how did it start?

Anti-Semitism, how did it come to be? How was it possible to have so many diverse people around the world have a common hatred toward the Jews?

Here is the ground work for it all.

Think for a moment as to what are the steps going toward the concept of contempt and group hate.

Generically here it goes:

Someone or some people have a concept that is generated either by themselves or an evolution of an idea. Then, there is a need for a leader (selected or otherwise). And of course, there is a need for "disciples," emissaries to spread that idea or concept. Once that initial small group becomes established or reaches a point it can expand beyond its immediate location, there is a need for an organization. It then needs to be grown, perpetuated and protected. The concept of religious missionaries came about as a mechanism to spread, convert and to accumulate more followers. More followers translate to a growing mass of diverse people that now have a common element in that concept (for the purpose of this discussion it is the Christian religion). Since the converts were from many cultures and people far and wide, the concept of a common unifier (Jesus Christ) was the New Testament as disseminated by the missionaries. Regardless of the versions being received by those far and flung cultures, the root concept of Christianity was conveyed and drummed in to those newly converted folks. Christians from Europe, Africa, the Middle East (or Levant as European termed the lands) as well as from far away Pacific Asia can now unite under that one concept. This was a powerful message to share even though all nations and cultures had variances of values, sensibilities or needs as well as their own internal issues and conflicts. The constant teaching that there is this central unifier of all mankind (Jesus) perpetuated the false narrative of his killing and the complicity of the Jews. And since the teaching in the New Testament is full of accusations toward the Jews, those concepts now multiplied in audience from a handful to hundreds, then thousands, then millions and now Billion plus people. That narrative is so engrained in the teaching that people from all corners of the Christian world had a common "boogie man" as was taught via the New Testament; the Jews! And not to be outdone, the spreading of Islam far and wide with its own criticism of the Jews netted the same results.

Now let's talk about fear.

As stated, fear drives humans to actions. The fear is either self-experienced or conveyed to the receiving person by others. When it is conveyed to the populace by authoritative figures such as government or community leaders or organizations, it quickly turns into "group think" because they trust the conveyor explicitly. If the messenger conveys hate or a target, the receiving folks can easily form into a mob. A mob needs very little encouragement to be driven to violent actions (a perfect example is the recent USA elections in 2020 in which then President Trump and his immediate entourage whipped up their crowds to the point of mob violence acts against the government, and ultimately attack the US capitol on January 6th, 2021).

Generic example of a manufactured hate situation:

Let's go through hypothetical scenarios:
The leadership has a situation on their hand that is not immediately solvable. A crisis event occurs such as food shortage, a plague, pandemic or the loss of a previous war causing a financial crisis. Often Kings and Emperors

run out of treasure and simply have no money to pay for their soldiers out on military conquests.

The next steps those leaders turn to is to simply blame others for their mistakes or misfortunes. This tactic is especially effective when the general population is impacted (such as a pandemic, a plague or even a loss of face). The weak-minded populace is told by the leadership that the cause of their afflictions are not themselves, not the king or government, or even nature itself, but rather others in their midst.

Too often in European history, it is the Jews they blame. Why the Jews? Because Christianity was a common denominator of all European powers (with a small exception of areas controlled by the Ottoman Turks). Regardless of countries or people, the church has become the central force dominating societal thinking and king making. Regardless of the version of Christianity, all have a common text that Jesus was killed by the Jews and they are responsible in perpetuity. It became easy to dismiss the real causes of events and pin it on the Jews; the "scape goat." This form of purge or bloodletting is as ancient as mankind. It has a "calming effect" to the afflicted. Sort of like breaking objects/glass. "You feel good after breaking things." After these purges are executed, all returns to "normal calmness" until it is needed again. Ancient Rome used that tactic on a grand extravagant level when they organized Gladiatorial and animal fights in the colosseums and arenas. They called it "Bread and Circus." Feed the masses and keep them entertained via the killing and fighting spectacle so they will not pay attention to the real problems.

A favorite of European Anti-Jewish acts was the libel that Jews used the blood of Christian children to bake the Matza bread for Passover. It was mostly used by the local powers to whip the uneducated Christian villagers and town folk. It resulted in a destruction or a murder of a few Jews or business around the time of the Jewish holiday of Passover (Pesach). I suspect this came about from Christianity directly in which when receiving communion there is saying of eating the body of Christ (metaphorically by eating a wafer of sort) and drinking his blood (again, metaphorically by drinking wine). New Testament (John 6:53–57) lays out this metaphor.[2]

This concept however can easily be twisted away from the metaphor they created and pin it on the Jews as if they too do it in reality, rather than figuratively. In any case, this was pure stupid thinking in which Christians did not understand their own scriptures. That then resulted in real violence by those weak minded prone to mob rule.

Inquisitions and purges

Expulsion of Jews within Europe is nothing new. In medieval Europe, England expelled all of its Jews in 1290. France did the same in 1306. Jews naturally fled to nearby Spain. Spain at the time, was a progressive empire that welcomed the Jews. However, as in many times and places, that was short lived. Religious tensions between Jews and Christians escalated to the point of violence against the Jews. An interesting narrative I came across was that the converted Jews (Conversos), were accused of being heretics because they still harbored some connection to their former faith and thus were unworthy to be Christians. Being intolerant of any version other than theirs and resorting to tortuous "investigations" (how nice, they just wanted some answers for their files, yeah, right!). The escalation of these accusations and violent acts that followed came to the attention of the king and he ordered an "investigation" to look into that (like he really cared about who is or is not a faithful Christian). It then evolved into an "official" endeavor known as the Spanish Inquisition[1] started in the year 1478. It was a more refined and institutionalized version of the Middle Ages inquisitions that were more of a free for all attacks on those "heretics" and the not pure Christians. Spanish king Ferdinand II of Aragon and Queen Isabella I of Castille used this religious turmoil to their advantage. They ran out of money to pay their debts to money lenders (mostly Jews). As a way not to pay back the loans, they and their Catholic church advisors, cooked up Anti-Christian stories and accused the Conversos of being disloyal and by association, the entire Jewish inhabitants in Spain. The accusation of heresy, Usuary, Anti Catholic acts, were easy to pin on them. Then under the auspices of the Dominican Friar Tomas de Torquemada started to torture and kill not only the money lenders and bankers, but subject the entire Jewish populace as a coverup to the King's aim. This action nulled the repayment and then wrapped it up in torture, forced conversion and the ultimate physical purging of Jews from Spain. In March 1492 Ferdinand and Isabella ordered the expulsion or conversion of the remaining Jews in Spain.

A side note: there are those that minimized this entire murderous event stating only 3,000 or so were killed (sounds like the same narrative Nazi deniers use in trying to minimize the events). These events occurred, that is a fact, and even if one person was subjected to this made up "investigation," that is one too many and it is directly as a result of the Catholic church's bidding.

There it is: The monarchy waited for bad sentiments to arise, and then with the direct participation of the church, pinned the blame on the Jews. The church carried out the consequences (torture, confiscation, conversion and murder). The masses were complicit by providing the physical support to the church. Locals were rounding up Jews and conversos and making their escape difficult.

Like any historical event on this grand scale, there are those revisionists that will twist and turn the event to their narrative (good and bad). There is a narrative by Catholic scholars that during the time of the Spanish Inquisition, the church actually saved lives by moving it out of the realm of mob justice to a more formal setting administered by the Catholic church. According to this narrative, the Catholic church's targets were "only" the Conversos. The ruse here is that the Jews were not the target. They "only" wanted to know if the Conversos were true Catholics"!

Any way you want to interpret it, the end result was a mass attack, mass conversion and ultimately a mass migration via expulsion of Jews out of Spain and into northern Europe, Turkish Ottoman empire and back to North Africa.

Some will spin this inquisition mayhem as a duel between Catholic Spaniard and European Protestants. It probably was wrapped up in the Inquisitions which were still carried out until abolished by the 19th century. But at its core it was an Anti-Jewish act. The actions speak for themselves. Jews were kicked out of Spain.

In 1808, Napoleon conquered Spain and ordered the Inquisition there to be abolished. It was not until 1834 that it was officially abolished!

A less elaborate scheme was the systematic and endless attacks on a smaller scale by Eastern Europeans (primarily Russia and Poland) in the 1800's. Those were called Pogroms. It did cause mass migrations again (out of Eastern Europe). There was no need of a royal decree. The message was clear! Jews were not welcomed in places they lived in for hundreds of years. Jews migrated enforce to the USA which was more tolerant of immigrants. Some started migrating to Palestine which was controlled by the Ottomans. The ending scene of the movie "Fiddler on the roof" shows the evacuation of the entire Jewish population of the small Russian village. The movie was adapted from Sholom Aleichem's book "Tevye and his seven daughters" describing the life in the small village and the relationship with the local Christian residents.

CHAPTER 13

Anti-Semitism, The New Age

We tend to hear the term "Anti-Semitism" quite a lot lately. In all forms of media. It is especially brought up during acts of hate or hate speech as well as vailed verbal references.

But first a clarification of the term Anti-Semitism.

The term Semite was coined in a racial sense by members of the Göttingen School of History[1] (Germany today) in the early 1770s when an active effort was underway to classify and segregate scientifically the different human races and cultural groups (they also coined the term Caucasian).

The term Semite was a European term derived from the old testaments book of Genesis: 5-11 identifying one of Noah's sons named "Shem" who is not Jewish (remember the great flood story?). However, it makes little sense as to why go there and not select Abraham who was the first Hebrew person and is considered the "father" of both the Hebrews and the Arabs.

The common languages in the Middle East were called Semitic and include Hebrew, Aramaic, Arabic, Assyrians and other variants. Jews are not the only descendent of Shem. So are Arabs and other inhabitants throughout the Middle East. Abraham is a descendent of Shem (many generations later), and is the father of Isaac (his mother was Sarah), whose decedents continued as Hebrews/Israelites/Jews. Abraham's other son Ishmael, born to him by Hagar, an Egyptian slave/maid/servant who went on to start the Arab people.

Now that we understand that both Jews and Arabs are Semites and share a common ancestral background of sort, where is the term Anti-Semitism used? Amazingly the term was first used in Germany in the late 1770's and 1800's during a time of "enlightenment" by European intellectuals trying to "scientifically" (read as pseudo-science) show the "inferiorities of the Jewish race." This was the presentation of "scientification" and justification of racism and anti-Jewish sentiments. The term Semite was coined and "science" was created to demonstrate the "inferiority" of Jews. The process of making Jews less than human or sub human took a hold. The perfect cocktail to stir up hate was formed. Religious bias where many Christians believed and blamed the Jews for killing Jesus, add to that scientific dehumanization of Jews, and now there is a perfect tool of hate. This now gave way to grander acts of brutality against a people. It then culminated in progressively worse events leading to the Holocaust as was perpetuated by the Nazi regime in Germany and their collaborators, enablers and willing participants.

Arab Anti-Jewish acts

Even though there were numerous Anti-Jewish acts in the Middle East, the term Anti-Semitism was not used back then to describe violence by Arabs or Muslims on Jews. Those certainly were anti-Jewish acts! All emanated from Quran passages that describe "bad Jews" in their eyes as tricksters, sinners and wrong doers in the eyes of God (Allah). The Jews rejected Mohammad as the prophet and Islam as the only "true" religion. The "bad" Jews are denigrated and described as dogs and pigs[2] and not human in Arab/Muslim world. It is a favorite of Anti-Jewish or Anti-Israel demonstrations and propaganda. The relationship of Jews and Muslims was fluid. It was good if Jews agreed with Muslim teachings and was bad when the Jewish minorities rejected Islam. And here we go again in which other religions are categorizing good and bad Jews as though they are the judges of mankind. These sentiments at times, manifested into random acts of violence. There is no equivalence in scale or magnitude to the toxic relationship that persisted in Christian Europe at the first half of the 20th century.

The fall of the Ottoman empire opened up the Arab people to move toward nationalism in which independent countries would emerge.[3] This process was first accelerated during the British defeat of the Ottomans in the First World War with empty promises to the Arabs. It then picked up further in the 1920's and 1930's initially with the concept of Arab royalties around the Middle East (as in Saudi and Hashemite families), as no one really understood Democracy in that region. Conflicts with Jews also increased in which perceived control by Jews in the Arab world was used as a propaganda tool by the German Nazis. As hard as it is to believe, the Nazis were sending messages of solidarity, Anti-Semitism and Anti-British propaganda into the Arab listeners, especially in Palestine. It proved so effective that Amin al-Husseini, Grand Mufti of Jerusalem and the chairman of the Supreme Islamic Council met with Adolf Hitler (December 1941). Again, the old saying of "the enemy of my enemy is my friend." But, were the Jews in Palestine really the enemies of the Arabs? The simple answer is NO! Jews did not control nor impose their way and were not in control or position of power over the Arabs. It was as simple as "kick the British out and take the Jews with you." There was no care that Arabs were also considered less than the German folk and that they too would have been eliminated from Nazi controlled territories at the end.

Political events that led up to the creation of the state of Israel in 1948 have transformed themselves into a religious and political adversarial relationship. Jews living in Arab lands were harassed and attacked physically and had little choice but to depart and emigrate out and settle in Israel. This new Jewish exodus from Arab lands was made possible by the creation of the state of Israel. Prior to that Jews were kicked out of one land, emigrated to another and then another, absorbing biases and acts of violence. Jews now have a safe place to go to; Israel. However, the creation of the state of Israel in the midst of Arab population became a new lightning rod of hate and especially after the 1967 Six Day War in which Jerusalem was once again part of Israel as an undivided city and the capital of Israel. A new call to the destruction of Israel (Jews) by some Arab regimes was popular. The rallying cry of "throw the Jews into the sea" was common propaganda.

public domain

Lately in the past 10-20 years, a call for political and economic isolation with an attempt to divide public opinion about Jews, Israel and Zionism started appearing. The Boycott, Divest, Sanction or BDS movement started taking hold in 2005 and continues today.

Code Pink activists pro BDS [4]

Divide the Jews tactic

Zion (ציון) is the Biblical Hebrew term for Jerusalem and by extension, the land of Israel. Zionism is a European Jewish movement formed in the late

1800's with a goal of creating a Jewish land in Israel (then called Palestine). The Zionist movement has nothing to do with kicking the Arabs out, nor is it an Apartheid system. At its core it is the return of Jews to the ancestral land of Israel. Politics and wars with the Arabs have tainted that mission. The BDS movement has attracted those with a "free for all" liberal sentiments tying Israel's military control of the West bank territories to Zionism, racism and discrimination. Israel is only seen as an occupier of Arab territories and not having any connection to that land. The same can be said about Arab and Muslim countries that discriminated (read that as Apartheid) against Jews to the point that they all fled.

There must be a finality of the current military situation toward a permanent political solution! But in my opinion even if the entire West back reverts to Arab control, then Israel proper will be in the same situation. The only outcome acceptable to the BDS movement is the total elimination of Israel as a self-governing country. Ceding control of the entire land of Israel to any Arab regime will just be an invitation of Jewish annihilation and another mass exodus. This cannot be allowed to proceed!

Finally

As long as there is a religious divide between Jews and Muslims, there will never be a sustainable co-existence.

CHAPTER 14

British Zionism and Anti-Semitism

British politics in the late 1800's and first half of the 1900's had a great influence on the fate of many Jews. Back in the late 1800's and especially after the First World War, there was an opposition to the Socialist movements about to sweep through Europe. The Anti-Monarchy groups that started sprouting in Europe wanted to throw off the yoke of the kings with their endless family bickering that grew into monumental wars, and have the populations participate in governing themselves. Of imminent threat to the monarchies was the Russian revolution.[1] Similar sentiments arose in post World War One Germany in which Communists were identified as the next menace. There was an interesting quirk in that Jews were singled out as the leaders of these movements (even within the Bolshevik movement). A kind of reverse psychology started to take root in Britain, which a "unity" with the Jews to enlist their help in fighting the Soviet Bolshevik threat after the fall of the Russian Tzar Nikolay has emerged. They cozied up to members of the Jewish Zionist Congress.[2] In turn, the leadership of the Jewish congress movement extracted promises (Balfour declaration)[3] that a Jewish homeland in Palestine will be granted by the British (the British victors of World War One), vanquished the Turkish Ottomans who controlled Palestine for hundreds of years prior. However, the British government was double dealing and promised the same for an Arab independent country. Even the British officer known as Lawrence of Arabia was duped into helping the Arabs toward independence from the Ottomans. The British government was not going to fulfil those aspirations of independence anyway. As history showed, the double promises were really not granted nor even intended to be fulfilled to either side even by the end of the British mandate in 1948.

British Anti-Semitism[4] was no different than the prevailing one in Europe and the United States at that time. However, Britain's agenda unlike the one adopted by the Nazis later on, was not the killing or destruction of the Jews, but rather the "soft expulsion" and to voluntarily depart Britain to their own ancestral land in Palestine. Thus, British Zionism[5] with a Christian twist and encouragement emerged. To this day Christian Zionism[6] [7] exists primarily in the USA! However, their purpose is loosely vailed. Its aim is to follow the Gospels, in which the return or the Second coming of the Messiah (Jesus) can only occur when the Jewish diaspora returns to the land of Israel, and then the Jews accept Jesus as a pre requisite, thus paving the way for his return. That is the ultimate aim of Christian Zionism because for Jews, it's aim is the elimination of Judaism as a religion.

Current Anti Semitism in British politics

In the UK, there was an election going on (in 2019). During the period before that election a Jewish Rabbi wrote a letter stating that there is a danger to UK Jews.[8] [9] Of interest is that a liberal politician (Jeremy Corbyn)[10] interjected himself in a divisive way. This politician started involving the Israeli/Palestinian conflict into British politics by calling Israel an Apartheid state and aligning himself with the Palestinian Arab cause. One may ask, why is it the politicians around the world love to hate Israel? And the simple truth is that being Anti-Jewish in any guise garners support from those brought up hating Jews. It also appeals to liberal and Social Justice minded people. Ask yourself further, why is it that these politicians rarely mention other countries or conflicts going on even today? Even persecution of Christians in those Muslim countries is ignored. Did you ever hear British politicians talk about ISIS killing by the thousands anyone not conforming to their version of religion? How about the conflicts of Hindus and Muslims in India and Pakistan? Do you hear any politician talk about those ethnic conflicts?

Regardless of the details or motives, Jews as a whole are again interjected and by extension accused in meddling and skewing British politics.

Imagine that! One Rabbi speaks and once again, all the Jews are lumped together and accused of meddling.

The shear act of even mentioning Israel, Jews and the conflict with Arabs in British politics is designed to segregate. You rarely hear about abuse, murder, displacements, ethnic cleansing by any other country or people.

I used here the topic of British Anti-Semitism as an example of "relatively" soft version of that hate. No large-scale pogroms or murders on the scale of the Eastern Europeans that were perpetuated. The sentiments were there just as the Catholic vs. Protestant conflict. Catholic and Protestant both aimed their hate and distain toward the Jews.

There were multiple versions of Anti Semitism in Europe, Asia, Australia, Africa, North and South America. All are interwoven in petty topics, greed, politics and using Jews as the common denominator of their ills. They all used Jewish tradesman, Jewish talents, Jewish money, Jewish knowhow when it suited their needs. However, when their usefulness ended or it was expedient to expel them, acts of violence ensued.

CHAPTER 15

Current Anti-Semitism in the USA

Us and them. How politics is used as a separator.

The advent of talk radio and internet channels have created a new and wider medium to spread ideas of division. Since the audience is already pre disposed to the speaker's thoughts, those platforms are used to further cement their ideas and indoctrinate the listeners as hard-core Anti-groups by using the term *them, others, those people* and of course, *Dems* and *Repugs*[1] to denigrate Democrats and Republicans. All these are terms used to hate and isolate.

There are two types of hate outcomes. In those circles of White supremacists, Neo Nazis, the results are the same as they were over the centuries of Christianity. You hear chants at rallies like "Jews will not replace us." Those are rallying cries to close the Christian ranks and remove Jews from their midst. Nothing subtle here. This notion was front and center stage when German Nazi party was formed and then again to consolidate its power, it needed a crises situation and once again blamed their woes on the "collective Jews." Exploit a crisis situation, create a scapegoat and then go after it.

Then there is the new mantra of Pro Israel in a way that singles Jews into separate types. Those that support the ideas of the Conservative talk show hosts and those that do not. I even heard statements from Jewish personalities that "You are not Jewish or that you are a racist" if you do not support their position. It is as though Jews need validation from loud mouth speakers on the political spectrum.

Here is an example of a Jewish conservative popular on social media in which he acts to separate Jews from each other based on their political leaning or his interpretation of who is a Jew!

Ben Shapiro: Why Jews Vote Leftist?[2]

Here he is separating Jews into compartments and even goes as far as labeling who is a Jew. He then goes into statistics of separation of "real Jews" from Secular Jews. Amazingly, this is coming from within the Jewish community. Why insert Jews into politics at all? Once again, all this just adds onto the hate of American Jews as non-compliant, too liberal, too leftist and thus it is OK to separate us again. I don't think that he realizes that by dividing Jews into "us and them" it just adds ammunition to all the Jew haters out there.

The reality is that Jews are such a small minority of world population (approximately 0.2% or 14 million total, 1% of the USA), that it makes no difference how Jews vote (either way Democrat or Republican). It is also amazing that Jewish personalities are now part of this division. Often it is embroiled in the politics of Israeli/Palestinian conflict and especially the boycott movement of BDS (Boycott, Divest, Sanction). Again, regardless of position on the matter, Jews are being divided from outside and within to the detriment of all Jews by being placed front and center of world politics.

Jewish politicians have to explain themselves as to their Jewish connection or heritage (Bernie Sanders and Joe Liberman before that). Christian politicians use religion as a Pro or a Con for their political positions. Some pander to Jews as having Jewish ancestry, or that hundreds of years ago, their family was converted to Christianity, or them having Jewish blood as though that makes a difference to their politics or political goals (example Alexandra Ocasio Cortez). All this attention is useless, but does provide fodder to those seeking to denigrate Jews as a whole.

At the end, it all comes down to what is the intent. Some have no intent at all (at least not overt or conscience) and just parrot what is taught to them. Some have ill intent and either act upon it, or incite others to act violently.

It is interesting, especially during an election cycle when listening to a political town hall meeting in which the audience members are asking questions of the politician. They often parrot the talking points of the right-wing commentators or worse, the racist talk show hosts as if it is absolutely true.

Not only that, often they are very emotional as though they themselves are involved in the specifics.

During the election cycle in 2008, when John McCain and Barack Obama were campaigning, McCain in one of his rallies took questions from the crowd. He handed the microphone to a woman and she immediately started saying that Obama is an Arab (with an obvious racist overtone that only a Christian should be running for president). McCain took the microphone quickly saying, "no ma'am, he is a decent family man." McCain correctly shut her down, but think of the situation for a moment. What if Obama or any other person running for president was a Muslim, Hindu, Jewish, Buddhist, Shinto, or how about an atheist? Is the USA the exclusive domain of Christians? Think about the engrained hate in a country that is supposed to have separation of "church and state." That saying rings hollow in which some Christians are routinely pushing for the USA to be a country run by Christians. And to go further, the racists amongst them saying America is for white Christians only. This is becoming the new mantra of Christian Nationalism in the USA.

Now, let's come up with a hypothetical scenario:

An event occurs. Let's say it is a suspicion of bribery.
A talk show personality builds it up as a crime or what is now the norm by placing a question mark symbol at the end. The idea is planted, but because there is a question mark (?) at the end of the statement, it gives the panderer an escape clause as if to say "I was only asking a question." It can be applied to any lie or smear. Is he an ax murderer? Is he gay? Is he a tax dodger? Did that District attorney just let a criminal go free, or how about questioning the mental capacity of your political opponent? The planting of any crazy idea is possible and the weak-minded minions just swallow it up and act upon it. Case in point is the 2020 election in which Donald Trump's sycophants started accusing election workers and even their own politicians of deliberately corrupting the vote counts, calling them names and publishing their personal addresses and phone numbers only to be viciously attacked and threatened by brainwashed individuals with death and maiming. Another

sinister form of hate that came up in an election issue, is that of one politician wanting to unseat a congresswoman in Wisconsin. That person actually stated that if her incumbent opponent is a traitor, then traitors need to be "hung up."[3] Later that politician emphasized that "only if it is true should the other opponent be hung." Basically, coming up with an unproven allegation, they planted a false narrative and condemned that person to death. Ask yourself, who gave the right to anyone to condemn another person to death via a libel? By what definition of a traitor does any person have the right to suggest this? And when was the last time anyone found guilty of treason against the USA was executed? The historical reality is not a single person! Thus no one in the USA was hung for treason. Other than during the American War of Independence in 1776 when folks were arbitrarily deemed traitors, people were only executed for espionage.

Then by extension, the allegation goes to condemn not only that politician, but also, their constituents for backing up a "traitor." I wonder if the next step in American politics is to accuse the political opponent of being a Jew, a Muslim or an Atheists. . . . Is that the next step (history repeats itself all over again).

An interesting phenomenon on the conservative media like Fox news where likeminded provocateurs and commentators always jump on the same identical topic all day long and sometimes many days in a row. It's like a chorus singing the same song at different octaves, but singing the same tune. The gullible listener who is permanently tuned to that channel, hears it so many times day after day that they think it must be true. Then that person(s) goes out in public and parrots that same false narrative. Before you know it, they challenge apposing politicians or government representatives or intimidate others in public with these same allegations or worse. All creating a toxic environment. Depending on the circumstance it does gets out of hand today and individuals are participating in violent and deadly acts (like the car ramming in North Carolina in 2017). A person was run over by an enraged/deranged person driving through a group opposing racism.

Another example is that of a rumor circulated by ultra-rightist circles (QAnon) that Hillary Clinton is running a Child prostitution ring out of a pizza parlor. Then an enraged person shows up at that innocent pizza place with an AR-15 gun (military styled semi-automatic rifle), threatening to shoot the pedophiles that did not exist.

Somehow, they are told that all Democrats are pedophiles; you hear the code word "groomers" as though the actions of others they do not like are grooming young children toward child sex or homosexuality.

Oops, I guess he was listing to "fake News"!

Words are a weapon and the easily-swayed individuals tend to act on it. But since "Free speech" is touted, nothing is or can be done to address it. Even hate speech appears to be protected.

Coming back to the topic of Hate of the Jews in the USA, these things do not occur overnight. They stew and flourish and are resurrected on a continuous basis. No other people are persecuted in that manner or level of intensity throughout the ages.

Even though the world Jewish population is less than 0.2 percent, there is a persistent perception by the gullible populace that Jews actually are much greater in numbers (some think it is as high as 20 percent of the world population), and that Jews and Jewish bankers control the world banks. Further, there is the faulty accusation that Jews want to control everything around them.

A resurgence of cloned speeches done by the Nazis in the 1930's is becoming prevalent. You hear today by some for example that the impeachment of President Donald Trump as a "Jew Coup." That's the same rhetoric as used by Joseph Goebbels (Nazi Propaganda Minister).

Here is an example of a Christian Pastor (Rick Wiles),[4] a religious personality hate filled talk:

Excerpt of his speech:

"The 'Impeach Trump' movement is *a Jew coup*, plain and simple. The men and women who are the driving forces to remove Donald J. Trump from the White House are Jews. America is in the throes of a political coup led by Jews. President Trump is surrounded by a rabid pack of *seditious, treacherous Jews* who are intent on overthrowing the votes of *millions of Christians who elected him in 2016.*"

In the name of free speech, he has his own media outlet in which he and his enablers hone in specifically on Jews and Israel. It is kind of amazing that haters latch on to the Jewish aspect of their target rather than on that person directly as though that person/ persons represent a whole people. Even though the chairman of the Impeachment committee is in charge, it is more important to the hater to publicize that he is Jewish. Ask yourself again, if any politician or even a president says or does something you do not like, do you say "Oh he is a Christian bent on destroying the USA?" The answer is no! No one is saying, "Oh that Christian Donald Trump is destroying America." No one is saying "Oh that Christian Hillary Clinton is out there destroying our way of life." Never! It only happens to Jews (and lately to Muslims); the haters never state that their target person is Christian. Why then say they are Jews? Numerically, Jews are such a minority, that even a concentration in one area or another does not overwhelm anyone. Since when did the United States become a country of only Christians and "conforming Jews." This falls into the narrative I heard recently in the North Carolina White nationalist racist chants of "Jews will not replace us." That narrative repeated long and often will manipulate and brainwash people thinking that the world is on fire and Jews are setting it (recall the QAnon conspiracy theory being perpetuated by some politicians that Jews have space lasers and started fires in the west). This is how a nonsense narrative gets weaponized and becomes outright dangerous.

Then Rick Wiles calls for nationalizing all media "since Jews control the media." I was kind of amazed at that same hater wanting to nationalize the media because it is biased against the then President (Trump). If you look back at Nazi Germany in the 1930's, the Propaganda Minister Joseph Goebbels (what a nice Jewish first name) nationalized all of the German media (including print, radio and movie industry). All then turned Nazi propaganda constantly to indoctrinate and flood the masses with their hate message.

Based on what I have seen and read, my conclusion is that even if there are no longer any Jews on earth, those haters will continue on their path and use Jews as a scape goat.

The takeaway here is that there is a connection between what Christians are taught when the New Testament is taken literally without understanding how and why it was written that way, and the consequent acts of violence.

The relatively new phenomena of anti-Jewish, Anti-Zionist, Anti-Israel movement and its associated BDS is a byproduct of the old hate mixed in with the advent of the creation of the state of Israel. Along with the desire of equality for all, what most do not understand is that Jews have no other homeland. None! Jews were displaced from the entire Arab Middle East region and North Africa as soon as the state of Israel was formed in 1948. The only place for Jews is the traditional land of Israel as established in biblical times. The advent of the state of Israel gives Jews a place of refuge. It is also a place where Jews can defend themselves openly. Jews are not going to be marginalized, deprived, used as a scape goat or slaughtered in their homeland. As hate continues, we can minimize its affects knowing full well that Jews now have a choice of where to live. An example is the recent attacks and murder of Jews by Muslims in France, England and the USA. Some Jews there decided to emigrate to Israel as a means of protection from those predators. The latest 2022 war by Russia against Ukraine also forced many Jews there to depart and emigrate to Israel as well.

Now the Arab Israeli conflict and Anti-Jewish sentiments in the USA

One can argue all they want against how the situation between Arabs and Israelis is unfair, and there are plenty of examples of cruelty, abuse and wrong doing. However, those same Human Rights minded people and activists are hardly critical of the way Jews are treated in any other country. Liberal thinkers need to be condemning attacks on Synagogues or Jewish businesses just as much if they want to be "fair." It is always one sided. Wars by Israel on terrorist or retaliations for thousands of missiles raining on civilian Israeli population are openly condemned as being unfair (recent Gaza war). Gaza is not even controlled nor governed by Israel. It is run by an Islamic hardline organization (Hamas) that advocates the destruction of all Jews in Israel and routinely involved in the launching of those missiles across the border. I don't hear those liberal minded people on how unfair it is to kill Israeli civilians! The situation there has to be addressed by the Israeli government, Palestinians and other neighboring Arab countries. It is more than a simple Human Rights issue. All parties must be willing to solve the situation. Otherwise, it will continue in perpetuity. Lastly, it needs to be understood that Israel is the only speck on earth where Jews can and have resided for centuries, but mostly under the control and subjugation of other nations. Arabs and Israelis can and should solve the issue of living together. One state Co-existing (most unlikely) or two state solution is up to the locals to resolve. I am sure that when the day does arrive and there is a suitable solution, there will still be haters that will use Jews as a lightning rod to further their agendas.

Al-Jazira (An Arab Gulf state supported media) did a segment on American pornography.[5] In that, they claim that pornography in the USA was created and controlled by Jews? Really, all Jews are into Pornography and all Jews are polluting the world sensibilities with inappropriate sexual deviancy? I was amazed! The next line is more amazing and it "quotes" some Jewish porn actors as doing it because they (being Jews) hate Christ and want to pollute Christians. It goes after the same narrative that Hollywood is also controlled by Jews. All that from an angle of hate rather than objectivity. And then again lumping all Jews into those categories.

You mean that if you have a Porn star that is Jewish, then it is a Jewish conspiracy? However, if the porn star is not Jewish, then it is just porn and nothing else? Jews do not lump all non-Jews into the Porno categories, why even discuss it as a Jewish occupation? Talk about the actors and folks involved in that profession. Do not lump an entire group into this. Pornography and sex are as old as mankind. Jews did not invent it nor created it in any part of the world. That Jews participate in Pornography is no different than any other human being. Sex and depiction of sexual acts are not the domain of Jews only.

Finally, the term "Fake News" has emerged in recent US politics (by Donald Trump and his minions) and is lumped with anything and anybody apposing their views as fake and manipulators (right or wrong or indifferent). This is a byproduct of free speech and is used to separate "us from them." The argument that those hate mongers and their followers hide behind "Free Speech" is that they can say anything, good, bad, real, imagined, conjured, outright lies and open hate speech. I personally have encountered recently that argument on a professional website (LinkedIn) which is a forum for professionals to discuss work related, job searches etc. . . . topics. Now a days, it has been tainted with everyone's political, religious diatribe. The mere mention that this is the wrong forum for these topics is met with "don't tell me what I can and cannot say." It is usually stated with venom.

CHAPTER 16

Atheism and Jews

Regardless of one's beliefs in the existence of God or if biblical events really did or did not happen, there is somewhat of a danger of negative consequences to Jews in particular when the prime objective is historical verification of these biblical events. Let me expand on this a bit. The Old Testament (Jewish bible), is replete with stories of events. Some for example are not unique but rather shared amongst other cultures in the middle east (like Noah's ark and the great flood).[1] [2] There are also various descriptions of the exodus of Jews from Egypt with some stating there is no evidence this occurred. However, there is a whole people that identify themselves as Jews and are the recipient of these beliefs. To them the written words as described in those writings along with cultural rituals defines them and their lives to various degrees (non-practicing to ultra-orthodox Haredim Jews).

The point is not to justify any religion or even a race since it is immaterial to the fact that over the centuries, people that have identified themselves as Jews faced constant persecution. Since the bulk of those persecutions were done in the name of religion (Christianity primarily), it also spilled over to those regimes that rejected religion altogether.

A case in point is the Soviet Union in which early proponents of Atheism, Socialism and Communism were individual Jews fighting for social justice. The approach those human rights people took was to form organizations that espoused equality and inclusiveness regardless of religion or ethnicity. The bad side effect was that when non-Jews were in a position of power, their old indoctrination and teaching came right up to the surface and Anti-Semitism became somewhat of a factor to kick out the Jews from positions of decision making.

The Jews that participated in national social issues were not religious. Far from it! They were driven by the need to remove oppressive royal regimes in Russia and Europe. However, those individuals knew very well that they are non-practicing Jews and moreover, they knew that their colleagues knew that they were Jewish. Regardless of their political identity or social justice objectives, they had an invisible label on their back as a Jew.

Granted, there were terrible examples in which those secular Jewish figures committed crimes in the name of their movement. One that comes to mind is Leon Trotsky.[3] Trotsky was one of the three powerful founding leaders of the Soviet Communist party[4] (Lenin and Stalin were the other two). The approach that the party took was more like a Mafia approach that included intimidation, maiming of opponents and outright murder of anyone standing in their way. It was all a "game of thrones" to see who will run the party. Trotsky was kicked out of Russia by Stalin, and ultimately murdered in Cuba. In addition to the internal power struggle, Trotsky was a marked man from the beginning just by being Jewish (Russian language identifies Jews as "еврейский" or Hebrews). At the first sign of political struggle, his religion was brought to the fore as a means of reducing his stance in the party and slowly justifying his removal. Notice no one ever accused Stalin or Lenin as "Oh, those bad Christian Communist"!

The Russian revolution outcome and the rise of Communism[4] has long been characterized in the west as some sort of a Jewish plot at worse, or a need to align with the Jews to fight it. Karl Marx[5] was a non-practicing German Jew who studied social issues and proposed ways of improving lives. His works and theories culminated in a movement called Marxism.

The main objective of those movements was not to denigrate, but rather propose alternate ways that are socially equitable. However, humans as they are, become greedy and selfish and corrupt anything including those that espouse equality. Now you can argue all you want that this is just an excuse to replace something bad with something worse and culminate in dictatorship, but unfortunately, that is the connections that Anti-Semites made between Jews as a people and Socialism/Communism. What is ignored is that Jews like any other people strive for equality, peace, justice and opportunities. Jews are brought up to practice "Tikun Olam" or repairing the world. Not that the world can be fixed by a handful of people, but rather have one do what they can starting in their own community. Even secular Jews are aware of this.

This is no different than any other society in which someone comes up with an idea to make things better. Social Justice is pursued when people are subjugated and exploited by monarchies and despots. However, when it turns terribly wrong as was with Communism, people are looking for where is the Jew in this?

Jews were always a visible minority in any place they resided (Jewish quarters or ghettos).[6] In places where allowed, Jews entered politics, law, military and government. In any country they resided, they strived to participate. They did not subvert nor try to insert their faith (most were non-practicing Jews). When economies were working well, they were tolerated as contributing members. However, as in any politics, when internal discourse occurred, they were immediately targeted. Even though governments may not be religious, all submit to their religious bias. Example was the Dreyfus affair in France in which a Jewish military officer was accused of espionage for Germany after World War One. All driven by hate with no truth to that matter.

Another example is the prevalence of Jews in German politics and military prior and during World War One. Germany became ambitious and declared war on Russia and France and ultimately engulfed all of Europe and many allies in a horrendous murderous conflict. Germany was a monarchy at the time (the Kaiser was the leader). Ultimately Germany was defeated and a one-sided treaty of Versailles[7] was drafted that imposed extremely harsh conditions for Germany and its population.

The harsh terms imposed caused a massive downturn to the German economy. Grave economic conditions in Germany and also around the world, gave rise to the Nazi party which at its core blamed their misery on the Jewish elements in the government and military. Here you have a party that is atheist, non-religious and supposedly Socialist (did you know that the z in

Nazi stands for Socialist?) National Socialist German Workers' Party. Nazi Party, known as the National Socialist German Workers' Party, in German it is called the Nationalsozialistische Deutsche Arbeiterpartei (NSDAP), political party of the mass movement known as National Socialism.

The Nazi party rose to power and ultimately had full control of Germany by the 1930's

Once in power, they instituted restrictive measures against Jews in particular and other "sub humans" as they defined. It all culminated in the Holocaust with millions of dead. Deeply engrained biased anti-Jewish sentiments crossed into a non-religious regime with murderous consequences.

Now that we touched upon non-religious led governmental systems in which Jews participated in and some of the consequences, lets shift to the more scientific aspect of Atheism.

Regardless of the definition, Atheism (or any variation on that theme)[8] encompasses those that do not believe in a God or any god(s) as well as those that don't know (Agnosticism), and those that feel there is some sort of a power or energy out there, but reject organized religion.

The issue here is that there is a chasm between people of any religion and those that reject it. The danger that Jews face is that their entire religion is well known throughout the world (especially the 20th century). Since all the writings of the bible and accompanying texts are available to many languages, it exposes Jews to unusual worldwide scrutiny. There is no other text that is so well studied, examined, interpreted, misinterpreted or propagated in various forms to suit the intent of the writers and their intended targets.

For example, there are various passages in the bible that describe very specific events and actual places. The walls of Jericho, the destruction of the Jewish temple in Jerusalem, Har Megiddo[9] (did you know that Armageddon is the Greek transliteration of the Hebrew words of Har, meaning mountain and Megiddo, the name of that place?), the event written in the Bible, the last battle between good and evil before the Day of Judgment is to take place. You can go to those locations today and look for any evidence that may or may not exist. Since many of these stories can't be substantiated (like the exodus from Egypt), there is a tendency to dismiss them as just a story. The point I am making is that it is of no use to prove any of the points in the bible that Jews believe is true, untrue or historically correct or not. The sheer fact that it is associated with Jews is enough to make Jews a target. No better example are people that are extremely active in social justice and are quick to interject themselves in foreign issues. That example is currently playing itself in territories that are under Israeli control but are disputed by various countries around the world, the United Nations organization and local inhabitants. Some people see Israel as the occupier and subjugator of Arab Palestinians lands dating back to both the war of independence in 1948 and more poignantly after the Six Day War in 1967. While one can look at this situation through the lens of who is subjugating who, it is easy to dismiss how we got here, nor how to resolve this conflict. Increasingly you hear about the connection made of Israel to Apartheid rule as was practiced in South Africa until the release of Nelson Mandela. Amazingly, we even hear that Israel is "practicing the same methods as the Nazis and is embarking on ethnic cleansing and mass murder." None of which is true! Again, as I repeated in other sections of this book, the only solution to the Arab Israeli conflict is direct negotiation between those parties and not through misinformation or grand misstatements.

CHAPTER 17

Conversion, Missionaries and Proselytizing

Looking thru videos posted on YouTube, I came across numerous postings of Christian missionaries, ministers and hard-core Christian pilgrims' visits to Israel or as they like to call it "The Holy Land." What caught my attention are the religious groups[1] that come to Israel from China and Korea (I resided in Korea and Japan for 7 years working there and also traveled to China). They come there with the sole purpose of proselytizing the Christian gospel to Israeli Jews. They come all ready to let you know that the mashiach (Messiah) has arrived (Jesus) and then start quoting passages trying to convince Jews to the message of Christ with an explicit objective of conversion. They dare not travel to Arab or Muslim lands with that same message under penalty of death by those regimes. Here is my thought! Korean and Chinese are as far from Israel distance wise as can be. More so, they are culturally removed from Jews just as much. They themselves have been converted repeatedly by Buddhists and then again by European and American missionaries especially in the 20th century. China and Korea were devastated before, during and after World War two and the populations there were eager for some hope to rebuild their lives and country. The Christian missionaries saw an opportunity and offered hope in the form of refugee support (with the aim of conversion or at least acknowledgement to Christianity). On the South Korean side, this was an easy task. The leader and first president after World War Two, Syngman Rhee[2] (Korean: 이승만) was already an ardent convert to Christianity and a zealot. He made it easy for others to follow with preferential and favorable terms to those that followed Christianity (this was post Korean war). Missionaries poured into the country and found it easy to establish schools, food pantries and then find converts. Existing Buddhist religion in Korea became less important and was considered by some Koreans as inferior or at the least less desirable. Once newly converted Korean got established and formed their own churches and organizations, they became extremely zealot in their fervor to share their newly found religion. In some examples, they even became cult like (the Unification church[3] founded by Sun Myung Moon, also termed derogatorily as 'Moonies').

On the Chinese side, the Communist regime marginalized religion, conversion to Christianity was much more difficult. However as in North Korea, secret missionaries were able to penetrate and find willing converts. Those converts usually were always in danger of being discovered and persecuted themselves only became more zealot in their conviction. In North Korea, Christianity is extremely minor in numbers. However, once and if there is ever a unification, missionaries will pour into North Korea and convert the population there with ease. As for China, Christianity is a relatively small minority, however with Chinese prosperity, the government there is more tolerant and allows Chinese Christians to practice and by extension proselytize outside China.

Now that Korean Christianity became dominant, they became overt in their effort to spread their version internally, but more importantly, outside their land. And since Christianity as well as Islam rely and actually demand spreading their versions, they found it natural to go and spread their variant of religion.

Here is where missionaries and Christian zealots play a part in passive anti-Jewish effort and contribute to the narrative of hate. Christianity adheres to replacement theology. The idea that Christianity has replaced Judaism is stated in the many examples of the New Testament. As I stated before, the authors of the various New Testament books (gospels) had a clear agenda of moving away from Judaism as was practiced at the time and replacing it with their modifications. Overtime and centuries later, Christians believed that their message is right and that Jews were wrong, sinners and outdated. Their message can be paraphrased as "Jews killed Jesus, the Romans were just poor Overlord slobs that were manipulated by the Jews and that Jews needed to be punished forever." The book of Matthew[4] stating: "his blood shall be upon us and our children." At the very least they want Jews to accept Jesus as their messiah (and convert) so as to allow the second coming of Christ. This is it! This is where if it succeeds, Jews are eliminated by conversion!

The" final solution" of the Nazi ideology, the years and centuries of persecutions, Pogroms, blood libels, Spanish inquisition, Christian missionaries and zealots has one common goal. Eliminate the Jews by either conversion or outright death.

My opinion

Anti Semitism started when the authors of the New Testament embarked on replacement theology (take over the Jewish religion and replace it with Christianity). I even heard the term that Christians are "perfected" Jews as though there is nothing good about those imperfect Jews. There is some really mean stuff in there that deflects away from the Romans which were the perpetrators of horror in the Mediterranean and ancient Judea onto the Jews (Hebrews). That doctrine is still perpetuated to this day. When you hear trash talk today like "Jews will not replace us " it is a code for killing Jews.

The young Jewish Dutch girl, Anne Frank who was murdered during the Holocaust, was only partially right in her diary writing.[5] Yes, there are good people in the world, and those should be nurtured. But in my opinion a third of the human population is evil, the second third is prone to be swept up in hate and evil acts. Only the last third is good (I am using the segmentation for metaphorical purposes here). She wanted to see the good aspect of humanity in spite of the evil that befell on her and her family. There was no group blame of the perpetrators of the Holocaust. No blaming of Christianity for her plight. That is a main difference between the outlook on life she and many Jews have.

Anti Semitism takes place in the name of politics, religion, atheism, liberals and conservatives. What you see in the USA and around the world is the rapidly rising conversion of that middle third toward evil. All the 'free speech' you hear by the hate mongers is just whipping up the mob. I don't think that "Never Forget" will cure this whipped up hate.

PART V: THE HOLOCAUST

CHAPTER 18

The Holocaust

Prelude

During the early 20th century, political events, a Bloody World War One that ended up in an Armistice (cessation of hostilities rather than peace) and rampant economic depression created an explosive mixture on a level never seen before. It gave rise to a German party promising greatness by primarily blaming the Jews for Germany's loss of that war. That party is the Nazi organization in Germany.[1] At its core, it called for a complete and total destruction of Jews.

The steps taken were the same old methods used by mankind for thousands of years. Blame a minority for your plight, create false narratives and events, then pin the causes of the misery on the minority, then create an excuse to alienate and restrict that group. And finally embark on murder and wholesale genocide.

No "ifs or buts," no opportunity to escape, nor hide your identity or even survive by conversion. This "call" or new doctrine became what was the Holocaust, the total destruction by burning of a people. Absolute genocide!

Creating mayhem and Nazi martyrs

It is 1936, and Wilhelm Gustloff,[2] a Nazi was spreading antisemitic propaganda book *The Protocols of the Elders of Zion*[3] in Davos Switzerland is shot and killed by David Frankfurter, a Croatian Jewish man. The shooter turns himself immediately in to Swiss authorities and is self-identified not as an individual person, but as a "Jew against Anti-Semitism." The Nazis make a martyr out of Gustloff "Blutzeuge," German for "blood witness). Hitler and his circle of henchmen decide that this "Jew" is signaling an all-out assault by the "corrupt, polluting Jews" of the German folk, that all Germans must rise and remove the Jews from their midst or else "all is lost." However, Hitler is against the immediate use of retaliation for this assassination and rather orchestrate a state funeral and a vast propaganda event. He waited for a better opportunity to unleash physical retaliation. However, this event was added to the raft of Anti-Jewish sentiments.

A side note: David Frankfurter's father was identified by the occupying Nazis and was killed in a concentration camp. After the war David was pardoned by Swiss authorities and departs for Palestine which is controlled by the British mandate.

photo of David Frankfurter in 1945 Palestine. Public domain photo.

Jews, Jewish bankers and Jewish control narratives as a trigger for anti-Semitism.

The connections of money and Jews is nothing new. It first came up in early Christianity. Mathew 21:12 tells the story of Jesus coming to the temple in Jerusalem, noticing the money changers, he turns over and knocks down their tables.

The aversion to money, or trading it or exchanging it for "excessive" profit has now become a sin. There is even a term for it: "Usury,"[4] in which the practice of "unethical or immoral monetary loans" is often used as a rallying cry. Instead of going after the Roman masters of Judea, Jesus goes after those exchanging currency from the vast Roman empire to those coming to Jerusalem. Imagine that, If I visit the Vatican and want to purchase something, don't I need to exchange my money to the local currency! If it is a sin, then why have currencies at all? I don't see that as being a crime in any other society. When it comes to Jews it becomes a mortal sin! Muslims have a similar aversion to money exchanges and earning interest. There is no aversion to banks in those societies. Both Christians and Muslims relegated the "dirty" business of money lending and banking to the Jews as if having them handle it makes them pure? The slippery slope is the definition of "excessive or unfair interest." I don't see anyone or government going after payday loans charging 25% to over 100% interest today! This was not a Jewish invention!

German Nazi propaganda cartoon showing a Jewish banker gorging on food served by the then German government, while the German folk, skinny, tattered and poor are served a bone.

Those "Outsiders"

The Nazis used their Anti-Semitic sentiments to whip up a sleepy populace in Germany (and later in Austria and other conquered European countries) with the old narrative that Jews are the unethical money lenders (aka bankers) and are out to destroy Germany. Now it feeds into the fear that outsiders or "Ausländer" in German language Xenophobia,[5] are going to destroy them and thus they are within their rights and more than that, their duty to kill the Jewish menace from their midst. Of interest, is that Jews were not outsiders in Europe. They were there from the dawn of their expulsion of Judea by the Romans and migrated within Europe for hundreds if not thousands of years.

Does it sound strange? Apparently not, since it did not take much to revive the Christian stereotypical notion of Jews. "Jews are nomads, Jews have no allegiance to the country they reside in, Jews often conspire against their neighbors, Jews financially strangle poor Christian folks around them and actively undermining governments with instability and revolution (use of Jews as leaders in the Communist movement, Karl Marx, Leo Trotsky etc. . . .)."

If you already have a population pre disposed to that kind of narrative, add onto it an economic crisis, create and event (how about burning the Reichstag[6] for example, or murder of a politician), raise the rhetoric by increasing the level of Propaganda (Goebbels controlled all the media in Germany by then). Ensure that the message is repeated everywhere and is listened to by everyone (free or cheap radios for all which at the time was a luxury item), and you have a population that is pumped up for "acts of selfless defense of their values." Those now are either active participant in acts of violence via para military organization; the SA (Sturmabteilung, the original para military arm of the Nazi party) are standing by and not reacting to these acts. In addition, there were gangs of thugs that would terrorize neighborhoods on a whim.

The rise of German National Socialism or Nazi party.

The Nazi party came to power at its second attempt, not as a revolution nor a coup. It was by the manipulation of crafty men during the turmoil of the years following the German loss at World War One. It came to power by a political process of free elections during a vacuum in leadership.

The Nazi party[1] under the leadership of Adolph Hitler pinned the loss of World War One on Jews. It came up with theories that Jews undermined Germany and its interests that resulted in Germany losing the war. Old stereotypical reasoning started manifesting themselves into that theory. In addition, they conjured up Jewish secret world powers were conspiring to undermine Germany's recovery after that war.

The Nazis had plenty of made-up ammunition at their disposal. They identified Jews in the German military during the first war. They identified Jewish leaders around the world and Hitler wrote his now infamous book in prison titled Mein Kempf (my struggle), in which he goes into his rational as to what happened, who is at fault and how to proceed. That document called into action the doctrine of the total elimination of the Jewish race in Europe.

The making of a doctrine of hate and destruction of Jews

To legitimize the Nazi regime's aims, they came up with the Nuremberg Laws of 1935.[7] Nazi Germany employed "scientific racism' to exclude Jews from German society (remember the section I wrote about the "enlightenment" period? Well, here it is codified into German law).

Nazi propaganda chart delineating who is a Jew. (Wikimedia)

The culmination of decades of hate to Jews, slowly increased from mob attacks on individuals, shops and synagogues to more powerful government sanctioned attacks. In November of 1938, a decree came attacking anything Jewish in Germany. That event was called Krystal Nacht (night of the broken glass) because of all the smashed glass of Jewish businesses.[8] It was not only the physical properties that were smashed and ransacked with the graffiti "Jude," or Jew, it was also the murder of those caught up as part of this sanctioned hate command. This was perpetrated by the Nazi Brown shirts, the SA (Sturmabteilung) the original Nazi party paramilitary arm. They were the predecessor to the infamous murderess military arm of the Nazi party called the SS (Schutzstaffel). However, as to who or which group was the perpetuator, it mattered not to the victims. It was clear that it was state mandated action against the Jews. In addition to these actions, the witnessing population appeared apathetic to these events and did not protest nor came to the rescue of the victims. Many cheered on.

Smashed windows of Jewish shops (Wikimedia photo)

As an aside, but related, the Vatican never condemned the Crystal Nacht following that event,[9] nor any murders during the war. They were complicit in so many Anti-Semitic acts, discrimination and attacks over the centuries that they did not bring themselves to stand up to Nazi genocide. They were even complicit in support of the Italian fascist dictator Il Duce, Bennetto Mussolini.

Now we have a prelude[10] to annihilation and a Genocide of the Jewish people with the following:

- The Nazi government in Germany has adopted genocide[11] as its mantra.

- A silent German population that at the beginning was unaware of the extent, but was aware of the proceedings so far.
- A willing segment of the population that is in full agreement and complicit in the action of the Nazi regime.
- A state church that does not push back or defend the Jews as being equal under "God's watchful eye." German Christians are Protestants as well as Catholic.
- The Catholic Church regime in the Vatican that does not condemn this treatment of Jews.

Add the next ingredient. How to do it on a grand scale

Initially before the advent of World War Two, Nazi experimentation in death were perpetuated mostly on the weak and infirmed. Individuals in institutions afflicted both physically and mentally were killed by various means to see how fast that can be done. Amazingly those killings were done under the guise of being humane (Eugenics played a part here). Practices of administering deadly substances into the body by means of injections and gassing (Carbon Monoxide from engine exhausts) were prevalent, but were deemed by the authorities as too cumbersome or not efficient in the grand scale they were looking for.

The Holocaust

Where to do it? Lands and locations to perpetuate this genocide.
Germany starts hostilities in World War Two by invasion of Poland in September 1939. It quickly shifts to the conquest of most of Europe and then in a shift to the Soviet Union in the East after their failed invasion of Britain in 1940. That land conquest in the east was the physical manifestation of a policy called "Lebensraum" or Living Space. It's outcome effectively captured the majority of the Jews in the world. The speed and outright shock to the local population allowed the advancing German army and SS units to act unopposed (or with little opposition). As soon as control of a territory was established or the advance of the German military units

allowed, murder of Jews commenced. Most of the killings were done by machine gunning or use of small arms (guns and pistols). The huge number of Jews killed by guns is established. I have firsthand accounts by my own grandparents (both paternal and maternal who survived) and by my father who was severely shot as a child of seven years old by German troops in the invasion of Poland in 1939. It is immaterial to distinguish which arm of the Nazi or German army performed these atrocities. The dead don't tell and the results were the same.

At this point, the Nazi machine indoctrinated their members and perpetrators as simply doing their job for the greater German good. No thought was given that they are killing innocent noncombatant human beings. The mass indoctrination did its job. Nothing could sway them or even insert a sense of humanity to those that participated and acted in these killings. Far from that, the German military and Nazi regime was more concerned that their troops including the killing squads called Einsatzgruppen, were being mentally affected by so many murders, that alternatives were being explored. Those culminated in the mass gassing by a substance called Zyklon B of people in concentration camps.[12]

Once these vast lands were under the domination of Nazi Germany, they created a vast network of collaborating governments that did the bidding of the Nazi regime. Those governments like the Vichy in France, Fascist Italy, or the ones in Hungary, Romania, Ukraine, Lithuania and many more, willingly rounded up Jews from their lands and sent them directly to the concentration and death camps that sprouted in Europe. Those camps were initially in Germany (like Dachau) and then soon in Poland (like Auschwitz), Czechoslovakia (Theresienstadt) and other locations.

Concentration camps

Concentration camps[12] were nothing new in World War Two. It was a common practice through the ages of a conquering people to place the less desirables or what they considered outsiders in separate camps out of view of the population. However, mass murder in those camps was not common. Those camps were rather a holding place and exerting control on those interned with some killing directly or indirectly by starvation and disease. Soviet Gulags are also concentration camps without the "mass murders." Even the United States during the war went as far as deporting American citizens of Japanese descent into the those "internment" camps. No murders took place there.

Nazi Concentration camps made it easy for their perpetrators to act on their prejudice and hate. No one is watching the goings on in those camps. No one talked about the goings on. Torture, sadism, maiming, murder are now mere internal acts and are not visible to the rest of the population. No one was asking what is going on behind those walls or fences! And if you have a brainwashed population or are pre disposed to these acts of hate, then so much the better. Those with a sense of conscience or moral sensibilities are either squashed or fearful. They do not object even if those acts are right in front of their eyes.

When the perpetrators of these camps have the facilities, a passive population, a vast access to resources, all they need are the victims.

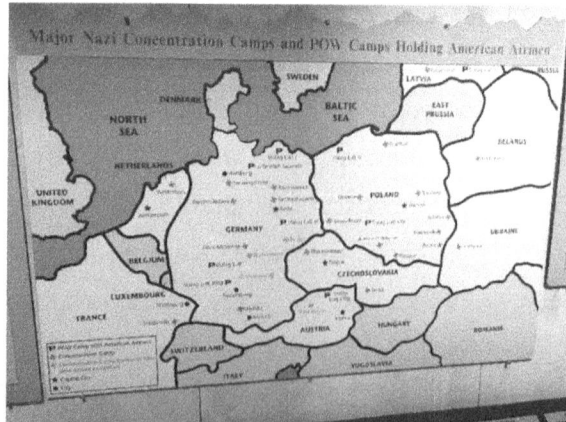

Nazi concentration camps. Photo by the author.

Wanton ignorance

When the Nazis set up the multiple camps, initially it did not garner any special attention. People did not yet realize what was going on there. Escapes from those well-guarded camps were rare. There was little to no information was available. However, it took no time to figure out what was going on there. Reports of mass killing on an industrial scale started coming to the allies (Britain and the USA primarily). Intercepted German Enigma messages were also coming in and the full extent was becoming known as early as 1943. The Allies overflew many of those camps and photographed them without acting. The prevailing excuse was not to alert the Germans then of this "intelligence." There were those that requested bombing those camps to allow some to escape. Nothing was done!

The camps had two purposes. The primary was the murder of Jews, but also others such as Roma (known then as Gypsy or Tzigane), homosexuals, political and religious dissidents and anyone else they did not like. The other purpose is to use the internees as slave labor. And when those people became exhausted and no longer able to work, they were murdered.

Murders continued right until those camps were liberated!

Public domain. US Army photo of Auschwitz

Author's photos at Auschwitz

Holocaust outside the camps.

Most people associate the Holocaust with the concentration camps. To them a Holocaust survivor is a person wearing a numbered tattoo on their forearm.

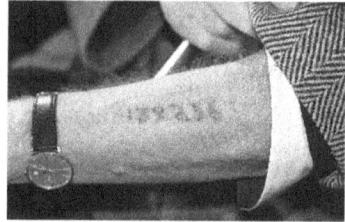

However, that is only the most visible aspect of the Holocaust. There were many that were murdered even before concentration camps were built. Some were murdered by roving murder troops, some by starvation, some were shot in the streets while being rounded up by the various police and collaborating governments arms. Many were massacred in their own town's squares and villages. Some were burned alive being locked up in barns and synagogues set ablaze (my paternal grandmother survived such an event). Some were murdered in roving gas trucks and cars exhausting Carbon Monoxide into the cabins where those victims were locked up. Some were simply pushed off buildings to their deaths. Some committed suicide or killed their own children out of desperation. Many suffocated to death during transport in cattle rail cars on the way to the camps. Many perished as refugees trying to escape the mayhem of the Nazi machine. There were endless ways Jews perished during the Holocaust!

Survivors

Traumatized survivors shared their stories. Some immediately and some after years of silence. Some never shared their ordeals or personal experiences; I know some myself that refused to share their experiences when I interviewed them. Both sets of my grandparents as well as my mother and father are survivors not interned in concentration camps. I was always exposed to their stories of escape and survival. My mother provided her video testimony to the US Holocaust Museum in Washington DC, USA.

My parents right after the war. Author's photos

My mother being interviewed while on a visit to Poland in 2009. Author's photos

PART VI: AFTER WORLD WAR II

CHAPTER 19

Zionism and the Return of Jews to Israel

Zionism is a Jewish political organization ideology that emanated in the late 1800's Europe. At is core, it addresses the desire for a Jewish homeland back in Israel (then called Palestine). The word *Zionism* has the word Zion (in Hebrew "צִיּוֹן") embedded into it. Zion is the biblical name for Jerusalem and by extension, the land of Israel. This movement recognized that no matter where Jews reside around the world, they are at best tolerated for their usefulness and skills, or vilified, persecuted or killed at worse. The search for a safe national home for the Jewish people lead right back to the land of Zion which was then called Palestine by Britain and Europeans (based on the Romans renaming Judea as a punishment for the Jewish rebellion). There were other lands under consideration as well, especially by non-Jewish Zionist and other Anti-Semites. Did you know that the Nazis proposed a Jewish homeland on the island of Madagascar located off the east coast of Africa?[1] There is no other land that Jews can claim any historical sovereignty other than Israel. For the last 2000 years and before, the land of Israel was controlled by many outsiders. Muslim Arab immigrated to the many places in the Middle East conquered by Islamic armies. That includes the land in Israel. Here is another dilemma. You have Arab people that lived in the lands for over a thousand years claiming the same rights to the land. The Muslim inhabitants were subjugated for the last few hundred years by the Turkish Ottomans. The Ottoman would not allow self-determination of the local Arab inhabitants let alone the remaining Jews that lived there. Back in the late 1800's when Zionism started forming, the power to work with was the Turkish Ottoman. Jewish Zionist even stayed in Turkey at the early 1900's to request the Ottomans to allow them a Jewish home land. That lead nowhere and the Ottoman Empire was collapsing and ultimately failed by the end of World War One in 1918. Noticing that there is a need to shift discussions away from Turkey and go with the prevailing power, Britain, Jewish intellectuals were working with the Zionist movement in order to gain favorable consideration for a Jewish land from the British government.

Events turned everyone's fortunes after the World War One ended. The Turkish Ottoman empire disintegrated and its extended territories were carved up primarily by the British and French. The immediate Middle East was sliced up along the new powers economic needs and ignored the population, religions or cultures. This arbitrary border delineation of the Sykes–Picot Agreement was a recipe for years of conflicts to come (to this day and probably hundreds of years more). The land known as Palestine was administrated by the British via a mandate from the league of Nations[2] (predecessor of the United Nations).

The issue with the Mandate is that it was still tied to the British and French interests in the Middle East. And as such, promises by the British to Arabs to have their own rule were made even before World War One when Arabs revolted against the Ottoman rule (remember Lawrence of Arabia,[3] Britain used Lawrence as a driving force with the Arabs to defeat the Turkish Ottomans). At the same time in Britain, Jewish Zionist were pressing the government there to support a Jewish land in Palestine. There was a document called "Balfour Declaration"[4] that "viewed favorably" of a Jewish homeland in Palestine. This was a phony way of appeasement to the Jews and really was an empty shell of a statement.

Foreign Office,
November 2nd, 1917.

Dear Lord Rothschild,

I have much pleasure in conveying to you, on behalf of His Majesty's Government, the following declaration of sympathy with Jewish Zionist aspirations which has been submitted to, and approved by, the Cabinet

His Majesty's Government view with favour the establishment in Palestine of a national home for the Jewish people, and will use their best endeavours to facilitate the achievement of this object, it being clearly understood that nothing shall be done which may prejudice the civil and religious rights of existing non-Jewish communities in Palestine, or the rights and political status enjoyed by Jews in any other country"

I should be grateful if you would bring this declaration to the knowledge of the Zionist Federation.

Balfour declaration

The problem was that the British never fulfilled (nor intended) their promises to either side and actually created an adversarial atmosphere between the Jews and Arab inhabitants of Palestine. Major clashes were taking place and some of the wrath was directed against the local British military (including terror attacks by the Stern gang). Jewish emigration to Palestine was restricted and halted by the British regime in order to contain the Jewish/Arab/British clashes. Illegal emigration did continue mainly by ships from Europe beaching themselves on the shores.

Pre Zionism-Jewish emigration to Palestine.

Prior to the British control after World War One, some European Jews did purchase lands in Palestine going back to the 1800's. There was a period called Second Aliyah"[5] in which Jewish emigration to Palestine from 1905 to 1914 took place. More small-scale emigration too place and continued till Israel's independence in 1948. Those lands were purchased from the local Arab inhabitants. I don't think that the aim at that time was to form a Jewish homeland, but rather find a safer place to live in ancestral Israel and away from all the Pogroms (attacks on Jews) that were common in Russia and Eastern Europe at the time. They formed small agricultural themed communities called a Kibbutz (meaning a collection or gathering in Hebrew). These collectives were self-contained and formed self-defense units to protect themselves from marauders and attackers. Jews lived in the cities as they did for the past thousand's years. There were variety of communities Jews resided in Palestine under both Ottoman and British rules.

It should be noted that Zionism emerged at the end of the 1800's which still coincides with European colonialism. There really were no independent countries then, and almost every land was part of someone else's empire. The most you could get in those days was a self-governing land but still under the control of the empire. That shifted as World War One changed the landscape away from big empires and launched nationalistic sentiments to form countries.

Zionism[7] became synonymous with Jews and Israel as a Jewish land. I don't think that the aim of Zionism was to replace the local Arab population, but rather increase the Jewish population by creating a home-land for them. None of the lands were conquered or confiscated prior to the war of Independence in 1948. This inevitably created friction with the Arab population with violent outcomes.

Side note:

The Anti-Israel narrative especially on the Liberal side is that Zionism is a colonialist occupying force (or the term "entity" as is often used). On the surface it appears like a bunch of white Europeans burst on the scene and took over Arab lands. Jews always lived on that same land and foreigners such as Arabs took over especially after the Christian Crusaders were defeated and pushed out by Muslim armies. Population shifts have occurred and continue to occur. Jews finally saw an opportunity to self-govern and also invite other Jews from around the world to reside together.

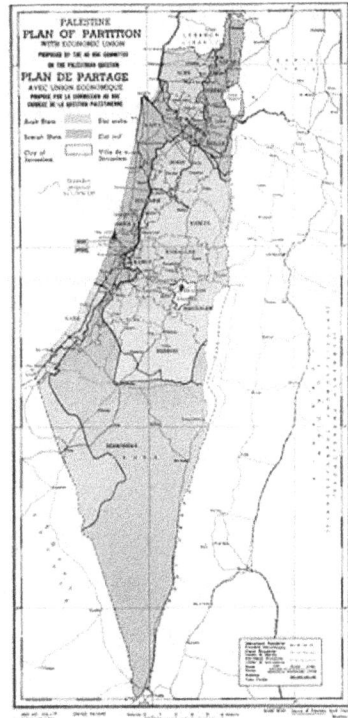

The entire situation exploded in 1948 when the British finally left Palestine with broken promises to all. The situation was handed to the UN to solve and the land was then partitioned[8] into Jewish and Arab states (via a resolution in 1947).

The Arabs never accepted a Jewish land in Palestine and once Israel got their

Blue areas for Jews, tan areas for Arabs, Jerusalem not included in partition.

independence via a UN vote in 1948, they attacked from all sides with the goal of regaining all the land given to the Jews and basically "throw the Jews into the sea."

Zionism as a wedge issue

Zionism is constantly vilified and is used as a wedge to separate Jews internally and isolate them with the aim of delegitimizing Israel and ultimately dismantle it. It is attacked both within the extreme Jewish Ultra-Orthodox community as well as a new form of attacks by Arabs and their sympathizers. Arab countries and Iran Islamic regime routinely attack Israel as the "Zionist entity." The issue with Zionism is that it does not offer the results that will suit all Jews around the world. Specifically, the extreme Ultra-Orthodox (Neturei Karta)[9] state that Jews do not need the land in order to preserve their Jewishness. They say that the Tora (Old Testament) is what binds them to God and that there are passages that forbid the Jews from forming their own country until the Messiah arrives. And since the Messiah is not Jesus, he never arrived and thus Israel should not exist and should be disbanded and given to the Palestinians. Since Zionism is not a religious organization and does not advocate for the religious Jews, Groups like Neturei Karta state that that Zionism is really an Anti-Jewish movement. Of further interest is that those extreme Ultra-Orthodox Jews have aligned themselves with Iranian government anti-Israel stance as well as Palestinians in demonstrating against the state of Israel. That is the Achilles heel of the Zionist movement. It does not speak of a Jewish land for all, nor caters to the religious because it was really a secular Jewish movement that was looking for safe havens for Jews. The ultra-Orthodox communities were content to live in a diaspora and explained away all the murderous attacks like the Holocaust as "God's will." However one looks at it, Zionism aim was to find a place where Jews (of any definition) can live in a protected environment. There was no forced agenda to bring all the Jews to Israel. The aim was the creation of a safe haven for Jews. Some would point out that Zionism took its message from Christians (specifically in Britain) that were more concerned with their belief that Jesus will come back to earth and all Jews will come to the land of Israel and embrace him as the Messiah and then convert them to Christianity. Amazingly, some European powers in the early 20th century embraced the concept of a Jewish home land, but the motivation was to get rid of the Jews in Europe rather than have them be protected. Even Nazi Germany dabbled with the idea of forcing European Jews out and into places like the island of Madagascar. Be that as it may, Jews were constantly persecuted in European lands and these Zionist thinkers (which were non practicing Jews) still had the Jewish culture in mind and were looking for a practical solution to these Pogroms and attacks.

It is immaterial to discuss how Zionism formed or why they decided that a land for Jews in Israel is the right thing. The reality of the times required a political movement, political negotiations, money and resources to come up with the solution of a land for Jews (again, regardless of the definition of such) and be able to self-defend and self-govern themselves. At the creation of Israel as a state in 1948, there was a huge deference and advantages given to the religious Jewish institutions in order to have them become a part of Israel. All matters of Jewish life are controlled by the Chief rabbis in Israel. Basically, Israel is run as a secular country, but is strongly aligned with Jewish religion. It is well understood that the Ultra-Orthodox in Israel are still having issues with the concept of a Jewish land at this time because the Messiah did not yet come. To a large extent, there is no opposition and in reality, the Ultra-Orthodox community plays a large political role in the Israeli government via religious political parties. Israel is largely a secular country. There are many non-practicing, somewhat practicing majority populace that is enjoying the protection and privileges of a full citizen in Israel. There is no religious test for being a citizen.

New attacks against Israel and Zionism

What many do not realize is that Israel and Jews are inseparable and that Israel is the safest place for Jews (despite regular attacks by Arabs, Muslims and their sympathizers around the world). Ignoring the fact that there is a need for Jews to have a safe place, can't be brushed aside in the name of so-called equality. Lately there is a movement controlled by Arabs/ Palestinians/Liberal supporters that labels Israel as an Apartheid country and an occupier.[10] [11] While there are certainly disparities between Jews and Arabs in the lands Israel captured during the Six Day war in 1967, those issues are primarily due to unresolved conditions and inability of negotiators to really solve the Arab Israeli conflict. As long as there is a military control over the west bank, there will be a continuation of fighting and mayhem. At its core, the entire movement of the BDS (Boycott, Divest, Sanction) Apartheid labeling, Anti-Zionism[12] has a single agenda and that is the removal of the Jews completely. There is no discussion of co-existence, or even sharing the lands. It is purely the old saying by the Arabs of "slaughtering the Jews" (Itbah al yahud/lidhabh alyahud in Arabic) and pushing them into the sea (as in getting rid of all the Jews from the land). Even if one supports that movement from a narrow social justice issue, they do not recognize it as a genocidal move against Jews, nor are they remotely interested in the welfare of Jews. There is no interest in inclusion ever. Bowing to these demands are just a suicide move for Israeli Jews.

Therefore, supporting this movement can't be tolerated toward any meaningful dialog toward a Middle-East peace, nor be accepted by Israel on its face since it is calling for the explicit and implicit destruction of Israel and the Jews in Israel. Arab Muslim tolerance of Jews was always tied to financial payment disguised as protection money. Jews and others that would not convert to Islam were forced to pay a tax. (The jizya Quran Verse (9:29): Tax Enforcement on Non-Muslims)[13]

And then, there is selective Anti-Jewish, Anti-Israel, Anti-Zionism movement when liberal leaning thinkers and activists insert themselves into the mix. The amount of energy poured into Anti-Israel rhetoric is very disproportionate to other regimes that actively discriminate against their own minorities. Example are the persecution of Muslims in China and Myanmar (aka Burma in old British colonial days). Or the Kurds in Turkey, Iraq and Syria and their fight for autonomy. Same for the annihilation of Christians and other religious minorities in lands that were occupied by terror groups like ISIS (Daesh).[14] There are many locations that occupy, subjugate minorities, but somehow those are relegated only small attention by those liberal thinkers, while Israel and the Palestinians conflict is front and center of many who only define social justice as a non-Jewish land for all. It is a continuously hammered message that is attractive to many on its face, but throws away all the ills that have been dealt to Jews throughout time.

The Bible and Anti-Zionism

When you hear the Ultra-orthodox Neturei Karta Jews anti-Israel rhetoric, please keep in mind that a majority of citizens in Israel are united in protecting themselves from persecution and have found that haven to live in. If folks start arguing or discussing the biblical context of the return of Jews to Israel, they would lose. The Bible is considered an authority document by some. It is replete in interpretations and can be discussed at nauseum as to its validity and directions. And then there is opposing arguments by Arabs and the Muslim world that God has punished the Jews as unworthy due to their sins. Basically, that argument on any biblical writing will go nowhere. Most Israelis do not adhere to the strict biblical interpretations and welcome the concept of being a Jew (of any stripe and description) in their own land. Zionism is an interpretation of both the return of Jews as well as a political and national necessity for their homelands based, but does not rely on a religious land. Relying on others never stood the test of time and Jews were always forced out of any land they lived in. Nothing is ever clear, concise, nor suits everyone. Remember as I discussed in the chapter of Who is a Jew, there are hundreds of shades and practices. Anti-Jewish acts have never sought to care about those and persecuted all Jews the same.

This is the Jewish Anti-Zionism. Then there is the two prong Anti-Zionism alliance in which Palestinian Arabs want to separate the political will of a Jewish state called Israel (Zionism) from Jews.

That narrative basically say's that Jews may live in Palestine, but not govern themselves and return control to the Arab populace. The issue of co-existence always carried a negative price for Jews. I hear it repeatedly that Jews had it better under Muslim controlled countries than in Christian (European) places. While that is mostly true, Jews were never free as full citizens for very long in any country. As soon as economies collapsed or a pandemic attacked a society, Jews were blamed and acts of violence followed. Saying that if Jews lived in Palestine under Arab/Muslim control will provide that peace and harmony and equality is shear fantasy. History is replete with examples of conquests, subjugation, coercion, forced conversions and restrictive life. . . .

Bottom line as far as Jews in Israel controlling and governing themselves as a result of a Zionist movement is a reality in which some Jews choose to participate. There is no forced migration of Jews to Israel and many have chosen not to emigrate there and some have left for various reasons (mostly economic). Those that want to wait for the Messiah can do so, but in my opinion, the messiah will never be recognized even when he or she ever does come, that person will be dismissed as a false Messiah and the same situation will continue for thousand more years. Jews in Israel do have their own homeland that needs to be protected at all cost and not allow another historical forced removal of Jews from the land.

Finally, I do believe that there must be a political outcome in the form of a two-state solution in which Arabs can also live adjacent to Jews. Some will choose to remain in Israel, and some may relocate to the Arab Palestine state. This is going to be an unavoidable outcome since Arabs will never accept Jews as equal as was demonstrated by the kicking of the Jews out of Arab lands post Israel independence in 1948. How this process is to be accomplished is not the topic of this book though.

CHAPTER 20

After the War Anti-Semitism

After World War Two, some of the Jewish refugees returned to their home lands (Yes, places like Poland and Germany were homes to Jews for hundreds if not a thousand years). That migration back home was full of obstacles. Some obstacles were the actual physical trek back in which great distances had to be traversed. Especially those refugees that sheltered in Siberia or farthest reaches of the Soviet Union. My father's family was sent all the way to Uzbekistan and central Siberia during the war.

Another obstacle for the returning refugees was that the cities and towns they lived before, no longer existed in any semblance of their former selves. My Mother's family was from Warsaw, Poland and by the end of the war, that city was in total ruin. No standing buildings, no infrastructure, no services, no food.

It was understandable that refugees did not have the opportunity to return to places like that. In addition, there was the psychological burden of returning to a place where Jews were corralled, starved, murdered, started an uprising and eventually were eliminated from that city.

Another obstacle for those returning to their places before the war was that those houses were occupied by the local inhabitants, for example, my father's family was from a village north of Warsaw Poland called Rozan. That town was not destroyed during the war.

Rozan

It became apparent that reclaiming their house was no longer an option or even viable. Jewish homes were reclaimed by the local Polish population that refused to hand over those properties back to their owners displaced by the war.

Author's grandparents' house in Rozan Poland on Kilinskego St.
Photo taken during the early 2000's (photo by Leon Zelazny)

In some places it was overt distain to the Jewish returnees. Open Anti-Semitism sentiments continued and did not allow for any smooth return. Returning Jewish refugees were rejected, not welcomed back by the remaining locals and were forced to continue to look for alternative locations. There were acts of verbal as well as physical violence against Jews in 1945 and 1946. Memories of mass atrocities were still fresh, but the old blood libels and friction with Christian societies have spilled into collective punishment once again. Nothing changed! Hate and collective assault against Jews continued. Pogroms and murder by gullible populace led to the continuation of centuries long treatment of Jews. A case in point was in the town of Kielce[1] in South Eastern Poland where an eight-year-old Polish boy was apparently kidnaped. After some days later, the boy appeared and stated to his father that he was held in a basement of some building. The father then took the boy to the police station to report this. On the way to the station, the boy pointed to a building stating that was the place of his captivity. On July 4th, 1946 the police and local militia went to investigate. There was no basement in that building and the boy was mistaken. Instead, it was full of Jewish refugees that returned from the war to have temporary shelter. The Police then escalated the situation and started dragging the Jews outside where the local mob enraged by old Christian blood libels proceeded to stone, rob and murder many of those innocent individuals without regards. Kielce was not the only post-war pogrom against Jews in Poland. There were others in Krakow and the town of Rzeszow. Those events went on without any mention or even acknowledgment by the Poles for decades.[2] The message was clear: Poland is not safe for Jews![3] [4]

U.S. Holocaust Memorial Museum, courtesy Leah Lahav

Relocation of Jewish refugees post war

It became apparent to many Jewish organizations and individuals that places like Poland were not going to welcome their Jewish citizens back. Hate in some places intensified even more by blaming the victims for the misery of that war and not the Nazis (as though the Jews provoked the Nazis to go about and destroy them and their countries).

An interim solution by Polish authorities for returning refugees (Jews and Christians), was to relocate them to the newly acquired lands taken from Germany. Those lands included large swaths on what was Eastern Germany (or what was Polish territory hundreds of years before). This border relocation was a product of the Soviet Union in which Poland lost its own eastern parts to the Soviets while gaining German territories.

A large city called Breslau by the Germans, was then "ethnically cleansed" of its prewar German population and was repopulated by Polish refugees (both Christian and Jewish). That city was renamed by its Polish name of Wroclaw. Wroclaw was a "clean slate" of a city to the Poles. It was emptied of its ethnic and pre war territorial boundaries that existed and therefore made it somewhat easier to relocate the returning refugees. New institutions were being established both by the Polish government, city government as well as social and religious organizations.

Old Religious sentiments persisted. As state public schools were formed, they welcomed all Polish citizens. Bullying in those schools were prevalent. Jewish students (my mother) were routinely taunted by Christian children calling them with the old derogatory of "parszywy Zyd" or filthy or contaminated Jew. Or the old stand by for kicking Jews out: "Jews to Palestine" was often heard. This was a verbal assault based on old teachings they learned from their parents.

The catholic Church did not intervene nor try to protect the Post War persecuted Jews on any meaningful scale.

Soviet rejection of religion and eventual migration of the remaining Jewish population in Eastern Europe

The Soviet Union espoused Socialism in which the secular collective by the state and the inhabitants was paramount. A competitor to state government was the church in all of its manifestation and denominations. The control of the church over government or even influence was severed; at least on the surface. All were equal and there was no religion to separate and divide the people.

Sounds great, right? But the reality is that religion was so engrained that no state edict can separate it from its inhabitants. Especially rural population that relies spiritually offered by the church. In essence, Church teaching with all its prejudice continued. The state did not possess any meaningful way of controlling Anti-Semitism. In Poland itself, post war, Jews did not hold any positions in their old government! Not on state, local nor any level. There was zero representation of Jewish population that made as much as 40 percent of Polish cities like Warsaw prior to the war.

Next phase. Another exodus of the Jews. This time out of Europe.

The combination of lack of places for the returning Jewish refugees, the rejection of the returnees, refusal to integrate them back into the society created a divide. A divide that was a continuation of prewar mentality, but this time Jews had to start over in safer places they did not originally come from. Two faraway places became those destinations. The return to the land of Israel (Palestine as was named then). The other place was the United States of America. Post war migration to those places was restricted. Eastern Europe was controlled by the Soviets and they had little interest in allowing any migration out of their new territories. Another problem was that Israel was controlled by Britain and migration there was severely restricted by them. Many were intercepted on the shores of Palestine and were then incarcerated in camps on the island of Cyprus until the end of the British mandate in 1948. The United States only allowed refugees in if they had any families there or had financial guarantees to ensure there is no burden to the government. Unlike prewar and during the war practice of restricting immigration to the USA, there was more of a favorable sentiment and more were allowed in. Financial burden on the USA was never an issue. Jews were always self-sufficient and never asked nor received any support from the governments. Jewish philanthropic organizations always assisted the new emigrees. Anti Semitism still persisted in the USA. Jews mostly resided in multi-cultural big cities like New York, Chicago and Los Angeles. Many successful Jews that managed to penetrate business, entertainment industries changed their names in order to blend in and be accepted. New venue of Anti-Semitism rose in which Christian haters accused Jews of perversion (specifically the entertainment industries). But that is a topic all of its own.

CHAPTER 21

Deniers and Revisionists

A parallel to the perpetrators of Jewish hate is the denial and revisionism of historical events. The main goal of that narrative is to minimize events against Jews as to paint them as liars. Worse is the fact that by creating an alternate reality of events, it gives the newer generations of haters the ammunition to continue their deeds as though nothing in the past really happened, and they are starting fresh in their attacks against Jews. You really need to ask yourself, why do they go through all the trouble of rewriting history? Why create doubt? Why minimize the horrors? Do they really possess any factual information to counter real events? What is the purpose of it all? The answer is simple. By creating doubt, it is easy to diminish a whole people and paint them as ones deserving these hate acts in the future.

Then there is the newer phenomenon of creating doubt formed by Arabs and their supporters [1] by stating the desire to remove Jews from Israel and eliminating it as a Jewish homeland. That narrative creates a false story, that those Jews that came to the land of Palestine, Israel today, are really European colonials that have no connection to the land. It even goes further by concocting stories, that European Jews are really Central Asians called Khazers that converted to Judaism, settled in Europe and then emigrated to Israel. Basically, denying the Jews their homeland in history, it makes it easy to deny Jews as a people and perpetuate further attacks (both verbal and physical).

Christian doubters and deniers

Evangelical Christianity shows full support of Israel and Jews. This is in sharp contrast of centuries of Christian hate and violence against Jews. Their aim is not to save the Jews, but rather have them converted to Christianity so their Messiah, Jesus will rise again. . . .[2]

As for doubters, deniers and outright perpetrators of hate by Christians against the collective Jews, here are some examples and excerpts from the New Testaments:[2]

—The Gospel of Matthew's insistence that "all the people" (that is, all the Jewish people) shouted to Pilate, "Let [Jesus] be crucified.... His blood be on us and on our children" (Matthew 27:25) led to the Christian teaching that all Jews are Christ-killers.

—In Acts 3:15, Peter accuses "men, Israelites" (i.e., "you Jews") of having "killed the author of life."

—In 1 Thessalonians 2:14-16, Paul mentions the "Jews, who killed the lord Jesus and oppose all people."

> "For you, brothers and sisters, became imitators of God's
> churches in Judea, which are in Christ Jesus: You suffered from
> your own people the same things those churches suffered from
> the Jews"

—In 2 Corinthians 3:13, "We are not like Moses, who would put a veil over his face to prevent the Israelites from seeing the end of what was passing away." Paul states that Jews cannot understand their own Scriptures: "to this very day whenever Moses is read, a veil lies over their minds; but when one turns to the Lord, the veil is removed." The Epistle to the Hebrews (Heb 8:13) goes farther: "In speaking of 'a new covenant,' he [Jesus] has made the first one obsolete. And what is obsolete and growing old will soon disappear"; the only covenant remaining is the one Jesus mediates.

—In John's Gospel, Jesus refers to the Judeans "Ἰουδαίος (Greek: Ioudaioi) as being "from your father, the devil" (John 8:44).

"You belong to your father, the devil, and you want to carry out
your father's desires. He was a murderer from the beginning,
not holding to the truth, for there is no truth in him. When he
lies, he speaks his native language, for he is a liar and the father
of lies."

This verse and others created a Jewish stereotype, common in parts of
Christian Europe, that Jews had cloven hoofs and horns (Michelangelo's
horned Moses added support). Well-meaning Christians have even asked
when did Jews have their horns removed?

The whole Jewish horn myth is a
mistranslation of the Hebrew word
"Keren" which is a ray of sun. A similar
sounding Hebrew word is, keren, "קרן"
which sounds and spelled the same,
but means horns, was substituted by
Christian translators of the Old
Testament. Instead of glorifying Moses
and by extension the Jews as to his
radiance of knowledge, the translation
now vilified Moses as an animal of the
devil's making. The statue is on full display at the Vatican with no attempt in
clarifying the image.

—In Acts 3:15, Peter accuses the Jews: "You killed the author of life, but God
raised him from the dead"

—Revelation 2:9 speaks of the "synagogue of Satan," although more likely
the people condemned are not Jews but gentiles "who say they are Jews
and are not," that is, gentile followers of Jesus who have adopted Jewish
practices such as Sabbath or holiday observance, dietary regulations, or
circumcision.

And finally, the ultimate statement in Romans 11:25-27 calling for the conversion of the Jews as a prerequisite for the second coming of Jesus:

> 25 I do not want you to be ignorant of this mystery, brothers and sisters, so that you may not be conceited: Israel has experienced a hardening in part until the full number of the Gentiles has come in,
>
> 26 and in this way[e] all Israel will be saved. As it is written: "The deliverer will come from Zion" he will turn godlessness away from Jacob.
>
> 27 And this is my covenant with them when I take away their sins."

The takeaway message to Jews:

The common theme from all these passages is clear to the Jews. It all is presented as: "We are all guilty in the death of Jesus, we refuse to embrace Jesus as our savior/Messiah, we are all ignorant of God's will and purpose until we convert and seek Jesus and thus, we are all made to suffer for these sins and transgressions."

All these venomous passages are written to justify their version of their relationship to God to the detriment of the existing Jews as a whole. It then vilifies the Jews as though their God abandoned them. These passages allude that it is the duty of Christians to exact punishment with the single agenda of replacement! And guess what? Islam has done the same. Instead of dealing with their own issues and directions, there is suddenly a need to vilify the Jews (or as they say, "the people of the book") as transgressors to God. Similar to Christianity, they claim the right to "fix" the Jews (this is an implicit call for converting everyone to their interpretation of a relationship with God).

Parsing of the terms and passages:

All too often, those with a sense of humanity will try to explain that "true" Christians do not hate Jews and go sometimes to great lengths to distance themselves from the haters. Some go to length of the Vatican and the Pope declaring those acts as non-Christian and that Jews are their brothers and should not be persecuted. There is also an interesting phenomenon in American politics in which Christians (particularly Evangelicals) invoke Israel and point out Anti-Semitic/Anti-Jewish sentiments as Anti American. As great as it sounds it places both Jews and Israel at the center of attention to a position it does not need to be. There is such a sharp focus on Israel and the Jews through the lens of the world, that is has become an envious and scorned country and by extension a politically charged target.

A denial of the facts that Jews have been persecuted by Christians is absurd. History is replete with examples of attacks, forced conversions, segregation and outright murder. Saying there is no hate against the Jews is just nonsense. Jews should not be collectively blamed for the ills of the world just as Christians are not collectively blamed for attacks on Jews. Unlike random acts, the Christian teaching and the writing in the New Testament does place a collective blame on the Jews for the death of Jesus and attacks on early Christians. If the cycle of collective punishment is to stop, (which in my opinion is a Roman deed to deflect from them and later by the Greek converts to early Christianity), I believe those passages in the New Testament need to be removed and those teachings needs to be stopped. Revisions to writings can and have been done since those texts themselves were written. There are many versions of the same texts that I am reading depends on who wrote them and which denomination adopts it. There is a precedent for modifications without altering the entire religion. Again, the need to remove these collective guilt statements are not to revise for some obscure purpose, but it is removed for being Anti-Jewish, wrongheaded and prone to interpretations that leads to violence especially those that believe in the literal written words (as in Matthew 27:25)

> "Then answered all the people, and said, His blood be on us, and on our children."

Who in their right mind would even say trash like this as to be punished forever just to have one person crucified by the Romans? On its face, this is pure libel generated by the Romans and early Christians which rejected Judaism at the time.

There is a similar type of treatment in Islam's Quran in which there is a narrative that Jews somehow "screwed up," are sinners and went against God and therefore God is punishing the Jews. Here comes the narrative that there is no other true God and his messenger delineated it all directly from God. Therefore, all others are just non-believers, heretics that must somehow be punished or converted to Islam (voluntarily so it says) or else put into a separate place. This is no different than any other proselyting religion. Both Christianity and Islam take direct aim at Jews and is using them as scapegoats. The minutia that Islam may make to differentiate "good Jews from bad Jews/sinners" is nothing but functions as a dehumanizer (Jews are dogs, apes, pigs according to Quranic verses) and a they have the ticket to exact collective punishment on the Jews.

Why both religions resorted to anti-Jewish rhetoric is primarily for replacement purposes. Both aimed at converting Jews to their religion and the old approach of collective punishment has been demonstrated as a successful tool over and over.

PART VII: HATE TODAY

CHAPTER 22

The New Reality in the USA

The years of 2020 and 2021 and for years to come

As of this writing, there is a fundamental shift in the USA in which hate is promoted in the name of "Freedom" and "taking back our country." This ever-growing trend is a direct result in which years of agitation by far-right wing promoters and hate mongers[1] are slowly repeating their narrative in the name of truth and "Freedom of Speech." Those narratives are often wrapped around conspiracy theories in which target people are dehumanized and characterized as less than human (sounds familiar?). Of direct concern, there is a strong support from many Christians and some fringe organizations and churches that basically embedded themselves in politics and are now part and parcel of the supremacy movement. Part of that political movement is once again the assertion that Jews control the banking industry and funding all these "Anti American" agitators against them (I hear it all the time when they mention George Soros). The current cycle repeats after successful demonstration by the Nazis prior to WW2 and is showing itself as an easy recipe to follow.

One only needs to see the attack on the US Capitol building which occurred on January 6, 2021. Amongst the usual Trump flags and banners were numerous signs of other hate organizations as well as religious ones. Specifically, a man wearing a sweat shirt with "Camp Auschwitz"[2] emblazed on the front as well as the "work will set you free" (or Arbeit mach frei in German).

Or the person(s) wearing a shirt stating 6MWE "6 Million Wasn't Enough," as an overt nod to the Holocaust in which 6 million Jews were slaughtered by the Nazis and their enablers in WW2.

And if you think there is no religious component to the mob attack, here is a picture showing them erecting a large cross on the grounds posing like the US Marines erecting the flag over Iwo Jima in WW2. "How patriotic of a gesture!"

Are we to believe that all those visuals are just simple symbols of free speech? Is that what they think a United States is all about? The answer they will give you is Yes, it is! Full stop. They are of the mind that they are right and you are wrong because their way of life is threatened by those "dirty outsiders." "Go back to your country they shout"; "America is for white Christians only" as they chant in various manifestation of the theme.[3]

Ask yourself, what is it that those supposedly "American Patriots" trying to message the rest of the US population here? Why link Nazi ideology, Anti-Jewish and racist propaganda to the American political system? Is it really that those rioters are being corralled by the American government into concentration camps? Is anyone in the government treating them as Jews were treated by the Nazis? Or is it the old narrative in which libels are heaped on Jews and whomever they perceive as outsiders pinning anything wrong or distasteful on them again? The simple answer is YES! They are again looking for a scapegoat for what ails them. Instead of demonstrating peacefully, they resort to violence, wreck the US Capital and then un-ashamedly pin it all on others. And as if that is not enough, the supporters of that mob especially Conservative politicians and their influencers say nothing about it, completely ignore it and worse. Then in a twist of disturbing sanity say it wasn't them at all. "It was those Antifa disguised as Trump supporters" that wrecked the capitol. It reminded me of a filmed comedy show "Live on the Sunset Strip" in which Richard Pryor's character tells a story where he is found by his wife in bed with another woman. In his effort to divert away from the obvious, he says to her: "who are you going to believe? Me or your lying eyes?." Basically, we are in the same situation today. People attack the US capitol in a violent way for all to see and is well documented only to have their enablers state it is all a fake done by others. You see the banners; you see the shirts emblazoned with Anti-Semitic blubbering and they still tell you "It wasn't me." If you are confused, don't be. It is the same trash talk that is repeated and believed by the gullible evil doers. Free speech at its core is a wonderful and good thing. Now a days it is used as a "license to kill" Literally. Did you notice the mob calling to hang Mike Pence (the then Vice president of the USA)? Was that really just a chant? No, it was a literal call for murder and mob justice. How about the hanging platform with the noose planted on the grounds in front of the Capitol?

Was that just a nice little decoration? Nothing subtle or covert there. It was a full-throated call for mob execution done in full display by people whipped up and "Swept up by Hate." And once again, nothing is being done about it. And despite all of the arrests and trials and sentencing done after the fact, not a single individual has been tried for hate crimes. No one is held

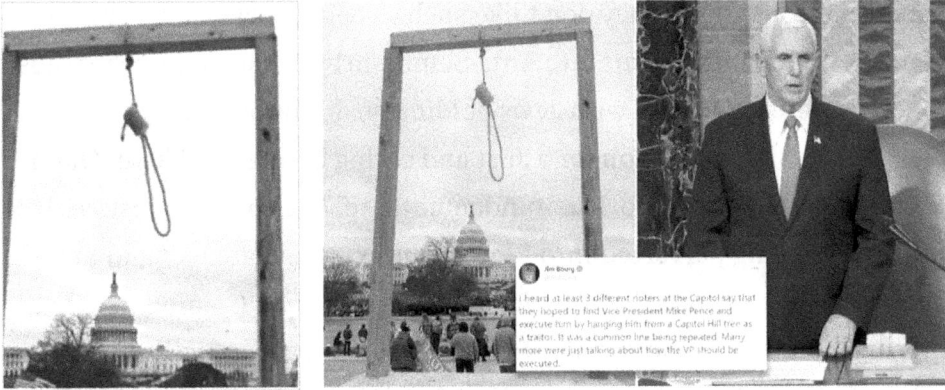

accountable for those words nor their actions. It is all Free Speech gone wild; even the then president Trump's tweet on that day stated: "Be there, will be wild!." You can say anything hateful in person, on the radio, on TV, on social media and it is all "protected" under the Free speech which is then twisted and redefined definition of the First Amendment to the US Constitution. It is a fine line that separates true free speech from hate speech. The unfortunate reality is nothing is being done about it. And then if any consequences are meted to the perpetrators, it is always after innocent folk are killed. All of the murderers that burst into synagogues and kill innocent folks have posted hate speech on social media. Some have posted long winded manifestos blaming Jews, Blacks, Asians, Hispanics for all the problems in America and the West. Talk about red flags, those haters are shouting from the roof tops and openly share their aims while hiding behind the vail of free speech. In the words of the writer Maya Angelou, "when people show you what they are, believe them!" We have it shown in full display with no or very little consequences.

Socialism, Communism and blaming the Jews again.

There is a narrative that is being hammered by all ultra-right-wing US politicians. That is the Socialism and Communism scourge that will engulf the USA. This has been demonstrated well by the Nazis back in the 1930's in which the burning of the Reichstag (the German parliament) was pinned on Communists. In reality it was the Nazis themselves that burned it and then pinned it on the Socialists and went on a rampage. Of interest to me is that by painting things they don't like such as being Socialist/Communist/ Marxist, the narrative turns into Anti-Semitism by the shear fact that those concepts were associated with Jews holding positions of power.

The Jewish aspiration for a Just and caring humanity "Tikun Olam,"[4] or the repairing of the world is fundamental to Jewish social justice. It is and always being perverted into "Jews want to subjugate us," and anyone that wants to help via social justice is automatically a Communist that is supported by Jewish money to subvert the world (you always hear of Soros and Rothschild which are Jews as the saboteurs of American and by extension, Christian values).

I recently had a lengthy discussion with a person in his 70's who identified himself as a Christian during the casual conversation out in public. It started as a simple friendly conversation. He then pivoted to politics and said two things that I had to respond to. It started with him condemning President Biden's cancellation by executive order of the Keystone oil pipeline from Canada and the 15,000 jobs lost due to it. He then proceeded to call Biden as a Socialist. OK, that was something I could and did debate him on facts, but I knew it was heading somewhere else. The next topic he brought up was the "China virus" as in the Covid pandemic. He now entered the hate realm which I was sure was going to come up. I asked him why call it as such? His response was that the "Communist Chinese government hid the entire virus thing" from the world (he made emphasis on the Communist). His point was that Communism and Socialism are to blame for this epidemic and consequent results. Then he said that the USA is turning Socialist under the new administration. I asked him if he knows what Socialism is about? He pointed that the federal government is going to take the policing rights from the states and will control everything. I said, "are you referring to the Soviet Union or Chinese style"? He said "Yes." My response was that those are totalitarian regimes ruled by dictators and will never happen here. His response was in the next 4 years, the USA will turn to one. I have to say, that I saw he was just parroting the right-wing media message that brainwashes the population. The next topic he brought is that America is not a racist country, but all you see is criminality and mayhem on the street (stating that those are all black people doing the destruction).

146

I asked him about the Charlottesville rally by white supremacists in which they were chanting "Jews will not replace us"? His response was "it is a small group that chanted that." I was a bit amazed that he did not recognize that the entire rally was by those white supremacists/Neo Nazis. Even when I brought it to his attention, he refused to acknowledge the obvious hate. When I asked him about former President Trump's remark about that event, in which he said "there are fine people on both sides," he said, "yes, there are fine people on both sides." I said "you mean there are fine Nazis and supremacists"? He then got a visual que from his wife and walked off without refuting that statement. He was just acting politely since he noted he is going nowhere with his conversation with me as I brought facts contradicting him at every turn.

That conversation solidified my observation that the USA is so hopelessly divided that there is no way to reunite and find common ground and that the white Christian folks feels it is under threat from "outsiders." You hear the slogans of "war on Christianity" parroted constantly. To them, there is no acceptance of different cultures (unless they "conform"). This is now taking shape under a new banner called "Christian Nationalism" calling for the USA to become a Christian nation with no room for separation of Church and State! One politician was even quoted (I am paraphrasing) saying that this nonsense of separation. . . . , the laws of the land need to follow the Christian laws first. It is so engrained that no civil discussions will ever be able to yield positive results and eliminate this kind of hate.

Hate endures, multiplies, denigrates and then acted upon in violence.

This phenomenon manifests itself in violence as in attacking Jews at their synagogues, businesses, homes, streets as well as the renewed hate crimes against Asians (due to the blame of the COVID pandemic on China). Hate based on irrational fear and the need to pin it on outsiders.

Neo Nazi organizations like the "Stormer" as in Storm Troopers love to pin everything that plagues America on the Jews.

Worldwide Anti-Semitism

Anti-Semitism is even more prevalent today as more and more avenues of circulating and delivering information is available. Social media is so inundated, that anyone with a message of hate can instantly become a promoter/influencer, and many take that information as absolute and share it further to other likeminded. Of special concern is that no longer is Anti-Semitism tied to Christianity and its desire to replace Jews by conversion. The creation of the state of Israel in 1948 has unified many liberal thinkers. They classified Jews as white invaders from Europe that colonized the land and subjugated the local Arab population into second-class people. This aspect is discussed in chapter 8 dealing with that conflict (The Islamic world and Jews). One can't dismiss the notion that the situation between Israel and the Palestinian Arabs has become a fascination for people from around the world. Many have no connection nor real interest in that situation and blindly follow the hate that this propaganda spews. If you look at the world map, there is Anti-Semitism/Anti-Israel sentiments in Europe, Asia, South and North America, Australia, Africa.... Just ask yourself, how is it that someone in South East Asia gets involved in this conflict?

Why someone in Africa would concern themselves with Jews and Arabs when their own countries are falling apart and people live in squalor!

Why not concern themselves with the murder and persecution of people in their lands. Why not identify themselves with conflicts of Muslim and Buddhists in Myanmar? Uyghurs persecution in China.[5] How about Christians and Yezidis murdered by ISIS in the Middle East? How about Muslim-on-Muslim attacks? It always comes down to Jews and nothing else? Heck, Jews and Israel are being blamed for homosexuals being killed and persecuted in Gaza?[6] Is it all a function of Jews? As if the Jews are the cause of all problems that humans create or cause. This is an old narrative being regurgitated over and over again.

Jews supporting hate

What I find amazing and short sighted is the number of Jews and particularly Israeli Jews that whole heartedly support former president Trump as a protector and a man for "helping Israel." Not realizing that the same love and affection they exude for this person also embraces the very people that would not hesitate to kill them all if they could do it. The idea that you can separate the man from the package of hate ideology is naive and foolish. It just invites mayhem later on. What is not realized is that being on board with a president that "rewards" his supporters by throwing them a small "carrot" such as moving the US embassy to Jerusalem (which is the right thing to do, but is only a visual token), or the isolation of Iran which is a big Israel hater and existential threat (and must be addressed) will lead to anything of real value to the Jews in Israel. While those are temporary and immediate actions designed for instant gratification, they will lead in a short time to the invitation of every Anti-Semite, Anti-Israel entity to act. While not supporting Israel is also not the right thing, the mere fact that it is associated with a race baiting American president and right-wing politicians will just invite dreadful results.

It is often that I hear Conservatives (Jews and Christians as well as Blacks and Hispanics) that they vote for Trump while "holding their noses." In other words, they do not like the person, his manners, his actions, but because he does one or two things they want, they will support him. Never mind that he encourages the same people that will later want to kill them without hesitation!

Covid pandemic and Nazi association

During the early days of the Covid pandemic in late 2019 and later in 2020 when the health crisis turned into a political tool by Conservatives lead by the then president Trump, it was first dismissed as a "Democratic party hoax." It then was dismissed as only affecting a handful of people. When it spread wildly, government agencies and health organizations started requiring isolation, masks and strongly recommend vaccinations, it was manipulated by the Conservatives as another example of "Government tyranny!"

Symbols of Jewish stars mandated by the Nazis during WW2 started appearing in a thinly vailed attempt to show themselves as "innocent victims" being marked for slaughter by those evil doers in power. This is so mind boggling to me. This caring government that wants to protect its populace is being compared to the Nazi's branding and ultimately slaughtering Jews during the Holocaust.

Painting state and local government leaders advocating masks and vaccines as Nazis was a favorite. As if those folks identified themselves with the plight of Jews.

You know this was all cruel theater! In the same breath, they identified Jews as the ones started this whole pandemic.

CHAPTER 23

Sports, Hate and Anti-Semitism

Europe is swept up in the old Anti-Semitism with the Nazi theme. Italy is in the midst of a resurgence of fascism and its baggage of hate. Jews are being singled out as targets of those groups. Countries that were ravaged by the Nazis in WW2 see a surge of neo-Nazis in the open. In soccer (also known as Futball, football) matches, you quite often hear the crowds chanting "Jews to the gas chambers," a cry to the Nazi practice of Jewish genocide.

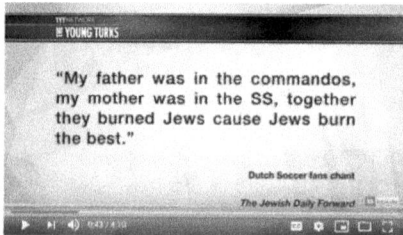

"My father was in the commandos, my mother was in the SS, together they burned Jews cause Jews burn the best."

Dutch Soccer fans chant

The Jewish Daily Forward

Replying to ▓▓▓▓▓

Roman Abramovich is Jew, stop supporting Chelsea

14:33 · 11.05.21 · Twitter for iPhone

There are no shortages of chants and it is all done in the open all around European Soccer. It is as though this "Bread and Circus" that Romans perfected to keep the population calm and content by killing of innocents in the arenas is played all over again. This time without swords, spears or wild animals doing the killings. This practice on the soccer fields is not unique in its attacks on Jews. It is perpetuated against African black players with monkey chants. Many of those Soccer Hooligans often vent their frustration outside the arenas as well and spread mayhem in communities. There is no shortage of words, chants, graffiti and placards. All it takes is at least one Jewish person on the team or an owner to get the mob going in its madness. Sometimes no Jews are associated with the teams, but is still attacked with Anti-Jewish chants.[1]

Poland, a country that suffered severely to the point of destruction by the Nazis is another place where short memories by Soccer hooligans and their enablers exists. Here is a headline from the Jerusalem Post in 2016:

Polish soccer fans torch 'Jewish' effigies, fly banner calling for burning of Jews.[3] Photo from the World Jewish Congress and other sites.

In 2014, a Polish municipal prosecutor in the city of Poznań ruled that chants by soccer fans are not deemed criminal offenses. So much for free speech and here we go again!

Ukraine is another place in which these messages of hate were apparent in European matches (although as of this writing in 2022, Russia used the false Nazi association by some as a bloody excuse to invade and obliterate vast swaths of that country).

Here is a photo of Ukrainian soccer hooligans unfurling a Nazi flag.

Incredibly, some of the players themselves identify with the chants, saying it has always been like that even when they were young. In their eyes, it is all normal and not Anti-Semitic.[3][4][5][6][7]

Oh, really, I say? You mean Jews to the gas chambers is like a nice little fluffy song? Nothing there but ponies and butterflies (sarcastic)!

Anti-Semitism is not exclusive to European soccer hooligans. It is all available openly in the USA related to sport venues.[8] There is a major difference in that no sport organization allows these types of displays and is quick to condemn them. On the individual players, though, it is treated with public condemnation and financial consequences. An example is an NFL (National Football League) player, DeSean Jackson, back in July 2020, posted images on his Instagram story quoting Hitler in which white Jews "will blackmail America. [They] will extort America, their plan for world domination won't work if the Negroes know who they are. The white citizens of America will be terrified to know that all this time they've been mistreating and discriminating and lynching the Children of Israel."

What amazes me is that here is a black person that should know better that Hitler was a super racist and bigoted against blacks as well, is being quoted by him as some sort of a messiah to the Black people by pointing the "white Jew threat to the Black." Here we have a high-profile sport player using his fame and followers to denigrate. His embrace of an Anti-Semitic black sect called Black Hebrew Israelites spilled over from his personal association out to the open demonstrating hate and venom. The Black Hebrew Israelite claim to be the real decedents of the Israelites and that the White Jews are just pretenders with their only aim is to destroy the blacks. You also hear that same narrative parroted by Nick Cannon, a black entertainer. Lately in 2022, the rapper Kanye West aka Ye has added to the Anti-Semitic noise and created a debacle when Tweeting "Deathcon3 on JEWISH PEOPLE" as though it is a military alert of DEFCON3. He then doubled down on a hate channel stating he loves Hitler. . . . A dinner meeting with former president Trump just added oxygen to his bigotry and Anti- Semitism.

What is apparent, is that no matter who you are, people with Anti-Jewish agendas seem to spill into many arenas of public influence. Sports, entertainment, politics, religion. . . .

CHAPTER 24

Hate in the Street

One of the oldest forms of protests and disparagements is street art and graffiti. This is as old as humans when they developed the ability to transfer thoughts onto stones and walls. While the transfer of knowledge and experiences into a visual form is a beginning of a civilization, it is also used as a media to convey vile and hateful thoughts and ideas. It is a cheap way to convey one's messages. You can carve it, use charcoal, natural plant and mineral based paints, spray paints, even blood. Then there are large posters that are printed ahead of time and then plastered onto walls. Haters tend to paint anti-Jewish symbols like a Nazi Swastika, or a Star of David crossed over. Those are applied to places of worship, cemeteries, businesses, homes, on sidewalks and walls. Usually, those graffities are not elaborate nor colorful. Primary reason is that the "painter" does it fast, usually after dark so they do not get caught. What they lack in artistry, they more than make up in the message they convey. For some reason, they are uncomfortable with doing it in the open since they know there is an element of wrongdoing in their deeds. They are not comfortable in confrontations, or open antagonism in public. It is more a form of a statement rather than an overt threat. As they

get emboldened or get away with it, those statements become openly antagonistic and start presenting threats.

Another form of street intimidation is toppling over of headstones in Jewish cemeteries or spray-painting Nazi symbols and statements over them.

Those acts are done usually at the dead of night by racist people. They are afraid of displaying their biases in public. Some graduate to spraying synagogues exterior and then there are others that take it further and attack physically the people inside. Those are the ultimate "graduates" of hate!

Of significance and importance, when these crimes were publicized during the Trump administration and was asked to condemn in public those acts, condemnations were lacking or slow in coming.

It is easy to just relegate those crimes to "young punks" or "drunken youth," but that is not it. This is an early indoctrination to the world of Anti-Semitism.

It was more common in Europe and at times in Arab countries in years past. It is gaining momentum and almost always, no one is held accountable.

Here is a street graffiti in Cracow, Poland. Photo taken by the author in 2009.

Translated from Polish:

"Jews, Jews
All of Poland Is ashamed of you
Cracow (with stars of David) "

CHAPTER 25

Words

Words are a powerful tool of communication. As powerful as they are, they get interpreted in the human brain based on the way they are conveyed and the way they were taught at home, schools and places of worship. Sometimes the words are overt, and sometimes they appear subtle or even as secret speak. This is common in every society where secrets are shared amongst likeminded individuals for the purpose of preserving that group.

Words are also crafted to allow for plausible deniability. Another way to look at it is that the words may have multiple meaning or completely no relationship to what they mean, but are assigned a new meaning.

A new example in US politics is the denigrating the Democratic president, Joe Biden. The chant now popular with Republican conservatives is "Let's go Brandon" Which started as a misunderstanding by a news reporter of the NASCAR crowd chanting "Fuck Biden." Now, the slogan "Let's Go Brandon" is fully understood as to its original meaning without saying anything overtly offensive.

Another example of words in which their original meaning was transformed is shown here:

Bad, that's bad. This denotes a negative, something undesirable and the opposite of Good. In popular culture, being Bad suddenly is a desirable trait that you want to pursue or be.

Another word to use is "kill," as in the statement "you killed it" meaning you did such a great job! So now an act of violence is suddenly a good thing. When it comes to Jews, the context of "kill" comes at a heavy price because Christians will put Jews + killers = Christ killers.

This came to full display when the then US president Donald Trump stated during the 2019 Israeli American Council advocacy group in Florida:[1]

Excerpt here:

"You're brutal killers." Here is the full statement:

"So, we're going to spend 2 billion, and one of them was going to buy a lousy location. A lot of you are in the real estate business because I know you very well. You're brutal killers. (Laughter.) Not nice people at all. But you have to vote for me; you have no choice. You're not going to vote for Pocahontas, I can tell you that. (Laughter and applause.) You're not going to vote for the wealth tax. "Yeah, let's take 100 percent of your wealth away." No, no. Even if you don't like me; some of you don't. Some of you I don't like at all, actually. (Laughter.) And you're going to be my biggest supporters because you'll be out of business in about 15 minutes, if they get it. So, I don't have to spend a lot of time on that."

Wow, here is a Christian president in front of Jews in a Jewish organization and still pushes the narrative of "killers" and money and loyalty division amongst Jews. Amazing still is that the retort to this blatant and open Anti-Semitic remark(s) is often treated as a joke, or something desirable. Like, you are so bad it is good.

The takeaway here is that there is nothing funny or cute or complimentary with backhanded words or statement. Those too are implements of hate!

The term "Jewess"

This is kind of strange when gender is assigned to a person of a particular religion. The term "Jewess"[2] was coined in the English-speaking Christian world to denote a female Jewish person. I am not aware of any other term used to denote a Christian, Muslim, Buddhist, Shinto, etc. . . . female in the English language. This is especially interesting (but will be obvious soon) since English is a non-gender language unlike French or Spanish. That term is also relatively new and depends on the person delivering that term, it is mostly uninformed, condescending, derogatory or down right Anti-Semitic. That term has also been reclaimed by some Jewish female groups to term it into a positive. However just because it is used intra Jewish people as a positive, it is still a negative primarily in the Christian world.

Think about it, there is no term called a "Christianess"! Or Muslimness! Or Hinduness! Or Buddhaness! The answer is that Jews are primarily targeted as a group for collective guilt and punishment. Even though every culture has derogatory terms for foreigners and others of different cultures and religions, being Jewish has a special place in the intensity of hate and is another tool in separating, splitting and compartmentalizing Jews.

Finally,

The old saying of "Sticks and Stones will break my bones, but words will never hurt me" is just BS. Words can and do damage much more. They incite violence on large scale. Their effects linger for years, decades, centuries and millenniums!

CHAPTER 26

Anti-Semitism in Movies

Movies have made their mark on society since the very early 1900's. This was a new form of media in which ideas, experiences and thoughts could be conveyed without the bother of writing and reading. A perfect tool for the illiterate as well. Initially they were silent due to the lack of technology to weave sound and sight together. That obstacle was surpassed and "talkies" started to take over in the 1920's and ultimately replace silent movies soon after. It was a fascinating time to experience something never before seen. Scenes of magic and illusions were favorite. A train coming toward the viewers who then scurry out of their seats for "fear" of being struck by the train is highlighted. Illusion is a powerful medium and serves not only to "bend" the minds of the audience, but also embed messages in a subconscious way.

The use of film as a means to highlight Anti-Jewish messages became a powerful propaganda tool and part of the Nazi state. It dedicated vast resources to that medium. Movies and roving visual exhibitions like "the Eternal Jew" and "Jud Suss" were the staple of Jewish hate in Germany prior to WW2.

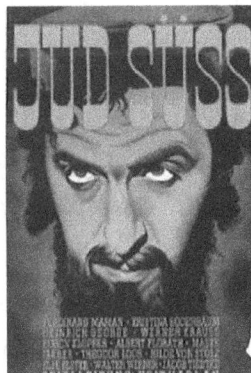

Posters of Nazi exhibits.

Many more are out there. This chapter will not delve into the many examples as this is not the primary goal of this book. Those movies prayed on Jewish stereotypes. Exaggerated physical features like big noses and pointy long fingers are used as a visual connection with what a typical imagined sinister devil may look like.

Antiwar themed movies

Another interesting concept was to ban and denigrate movies that highlighted Jewish topics or Anti-war themed movies. Movies like the 1930 Universal studios "All quiet on the Western front" were deemed by the Nazi and anti-Jewish sympathizers as Jewish propaganda.

Movie poster. Public Domain. Not copyrighted.

Christian themed movies

Then there are religious themed movies associated with biblical times at and around the Roman subjugation of Judea and specifically Jesus and the crucifixion. Those movies in which the gore of beating and abuse of Jesus by the Romans and ultimately his killing has the Jewish mob participation being highlighted. Specific examples are "The Last Temptation of Christ" a 1988 movie by Martin Scorsese, and then there is Mel Gibson's "Passion of the Christ" attempt in being authentic (speak in Latin and Aramaic languages) highlighting the Jewish "guilt" in the crucifixion of Christ.

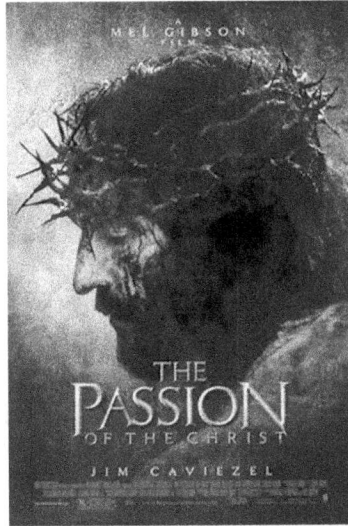

The movie is especially gory in the details shown on the screen. It attempts to create the lines in the New Testament implicating the Jews in Jesus's killing. Its aim is not to contradict the written words in the gospels as absolute "truths," but rather magnify them.

There are also the "soft" themed movies like "Ben Hur" in which the ultimate transition of a Jewish family to early Christianity is highlighted not as a Jewish struggle against Roman tyranny, but rather the abandonment of the Jews and "conversion" into Christianity.

Comedy and poking fun at Nazis

And then there are movies of sarcastic or comedic caricature nature against Nazis; in particular, Charley Chaplin's movie of "The Great Dictator" comes to mind.

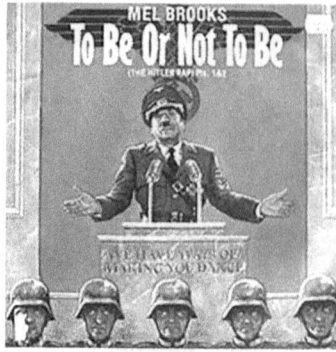

Mel Brooks was prolific in his comedies dealing with human social issues and Anti-Nazi comedies as in "To Be or Not to Be."

Comedy is often used as a relief and as an equalizer to the madness of mankind. A related World War Two topic, was dealing with German prisoner of war camps called" Stalags." During the late 1960's, there was a Television show called "Hogan's Heroes." Its main theme was the Allied prisoners (American, British, French) outsmarting and poking fun at their German prisoner of war captors as being bumbling stupid fools guarding the fictional "Stalag 13."

As a summary, movies are a powerful means of conveying messages. They can show historical facts or contort them to the will of the movie writers.

PART VIII: MY PERSONAL EXPERIENCES

CHAPTER 27

My Personal Experiences

As someone who emigrated to the USA during my teen years, I have to say that I have not personally experienced Anti-Semitism or overt acts of hate. At most, I have experienced hidden biases, but none penetrated the surface or hindered my life. I could credit it to the environment I selected to be in or the field of interests that I developed. Or I can credit it to my strong character that did not tolerate such discussion and none arose with me. My family including my parents and grandparents had first hand experiences of those culminating in death, destruction to property and forced departure from their homes during and after the Holocaust. I have documented their plight in a whole separate topic not in this book.

My wife was born in the USA and was exposed to some of these "soft" Anti-Semitic sentiments during her growing up years. In Florida, she was aware of sentiments that Jews were not allowed in certain places (hotels and restaurants or private clubs during the 1960's). In Connecticut, while in primary school, she was called "dirty Jew" and "Jesus killer." Many years later, she experienced casual statements by several repair persons providing service to a house we rented while temporarily residing in Montreal Canada in 2015. One of these persons was spouting that the owner is "cheap as a Jew" for not agreeing to perform certain costly repairs. A bit surprised, she stopped the conversation right then and asked the person to leave. The reality was that the owner of the house was in fact a Christian residing in Europe at the time! Words to inflate and blame!

I have had multiple discussions about religion with many people. I find the topic interesting and wanted to see perspectives others have.

Some of the discussions were educational and some were what I considered so indoctrinated in their belief, that there was no point continuing the discussions.

My personal discussion with coworkers

During the early writing of this book, I had dinner with two coworkers. They were visiting individuals from a European country (Poland) and an Asian country (India). The conversation in short order zeroed in on their interest in Judaism but really it was about Christianity. They asked with interest about Jews because I openly identified myself as one. Not knowing their motives at that moment, I started with the biblical story of Abraham and the concept of a singular god and the migration to the land known today as Israel. Then I talked about Israel and Judea being under constant conflicts and being conquered including from far and wide, like the Babylonians, Greeks and later by the Romans

My coworkers revealed proudly that they are Christians. Both came across as energetic believers. That apparently piqued their curiosity about Jews in general and me being Jewish in particular.

I then pointed out that the New Testament of the early church is replete with Anti-Jewish verses and statements. Those writing have been persistent throughout the early Christian teaching and perpetuated into modern day Anti-Semitism. To my amazement, their reply was that Christians do not hate the Jews because all Christians are decedents of the Jewish faith! Further they stated that those are misconceptions and misinterpretations of the writings. The conversation progressed into two paths. One is that not all people who say they are Christians are really "true" Christians (there were remarks about the Catholic church and the Pope), and the second argument is that the quotes from Matthew and Peter did not blame the Jews for Jesus death because they, the Jews, did not know what they did or were "ignorant" of their role in his death. I was kind of shocked that this sort of revisionist interpretation exists. I pointed to them that in the New Testament, Peter at one of the gatherings said to the crowd that

"You killed . . ." The shear statement, I then said to them, is that the writer points a finger to a mass of people that were not there, did not participate in the decision making of Jesus killing, nor even witnessed the crucifixion. The "You . . ." is a collective sin of all Jews in this event. Further, there was a statement that the blood of Jesus will be upon us and our children. My point is that whoever wrote this and other passages, clearly intended to continue this act of vengeance (in their minds and intents) on Jews in perpetuity. My coworker's response was that I was missing the follow up and that God did not reveal the true purpose of Jesus death to the Jews. They said I really missed the meaning of the "prophecy." I said that this is all nonsense and that as thinking people, they should understand that when these teaching are perpetuated, people will make up their minds at the first part as to "what"(Jesus death), and ignore the second part as to "why" (god did not reveal to the Jews the true purpose of Jesus death). Their rebuttal was always about prophecy and that all those are coming true and will continue. Then they insisted that the establishment of the state of Israel in 1948 was God's will and prophecy. I had to basically say that they are so immersed in their beliefs and zealotry that they do not see the practical outcome of the acts and violence against Jews under any banner of Christianity (their version or not), nor that it is any different than any other attack on Jews even before Christianity evolved.

All this talk made me realize that Jews need to be separated from the Christian teachings, prophecies and be left alone. Do not use us as the reason or obstacles to your continuous evolvements, nor discussions of the Rapture, the coming of Jesus etc. . . . We are not your vehicle to any ascension to God. Those Jews today nor the ones before us are not complicit in Jesus's killing, we were not there, and just stop this guilt by association. Jews don't go around the world trying to convert anyone because we do not proselytize. Jews have not participated in any religious wars on other nations or religions, we were exiled from our lands, went to live amongst other nations, but rarely allowed to integrate in those societies. Jews were often segregated to their quarters (ghettos) and made to wear badges and signs that pointed out to the rest of the population that we are to be treated differently. Even as some rights were given to Jews, those were taken away at the whims of the leadership of those countries. When I hear apologists stating that Jews were equal citizens, the reality is that depends on the time and circumstances and those were fleeting at best.

As expected, the dinner discussion ended. I did not agree to their interpretations and came to a conclusion that stopping Anti-Semitism cannot succeed if we as Jews are part of the New Testament vision, since in their eyes, we are ignorant of God's plans and only when we as Jews accept their messenger on earth (Jesus) as our savior and messiah, will their journey succeed.

It is an impossible task to disassociate Christianity and Islam from Judaism since both are direct decedents of Jewish religion. Both are proselytizing religions in which conversion is a direct command (spreading the word) and is pursued by their institutions, their missionaries, emissaries and members by direct reasoning, influence and outright coercion that is often associated with death if not accepted initially. Libel is also used as a weapon, and is lumped into the category of blasphemy, heresy or outright attack at their sensibilities. So you lose either way. If as a Jew you don't convert/conform, you are a labeled a heretic or Infidel. If you resist or say anything then you are a heretic and thus deserve punishment.

And even though these were very friendly and pro Jewish individuals who would never participate nor condone anti-Semitism, in my view, their zealot beliefs only contribute to the propagation of Jews being a part of their destiny. The written words of the New Testament's and selective quotes from the old testaments in regards to prophecies as related to the fate of the Jews and their" vengeful" God, just perpetuate the notion that Jews are their objects in the completion of their religious destiny.

Years ago, I was working in South Korea in an aviation technical capacity. I and my family lived amongst the locals close to four years. We were not sheltered in compounds or exclusive expat neighborhoods. We have grown to admire the people and their culture and even learned some of the language. There was not a single confrontation with any and the topic of religion never penetrated any conversation. At one point when we resided in a high-rise apartment building, our next-door neighbor invited our children to play with theirs and other kids. The door to their apartment was open and after a while, my wife and I walked in to check on our kids. What we witnessed was a Christian bible teaching session. We then removed our children and told them that we are Jewish and do not participate in Christian religious activities. There was no attempt by them to revive this topic and our neighborly interactions continued. What struck me is that a Korean convert felt the need to recite the Christian religion to our family. This was another reminder that new converts are just as zealot and by their new devotion, they are contributing to the separation of people and cultures around the world.

Another encounter in Korea had nothing to do with the local folks, but rather with an American expat working in the same facility as I. During our daily lunch at the cafeteria, that person engaged me with a conversation about Christianity. His line on that topic was that at most, only 5 percent of those calling themselves Christians are "true Christians." I was somewhat surprised that Christians are now actively discriminating against each other's version of the religion. This was not Catholic versus Protestants, but is much deeper than that. As though only his definition is correct and others are just imposters. I asked him as to why have this talk at all? The response was just a mashup of old rhetoric and nonsense talk. When a zealot talks, that person elevates themselves above all and proceeds as though they have exclusive right to categorize and catalog the "true message" of Christianity. That conversation went nowhere and I decided no good will come of this and stopped meeting him at lunch.

More personal encounters

שָׂרָה A while ago, I visited a Senior Living facility with my mother. She was wearing a necklace with her Hebrew name, Sarah.

Mom also wore the old superstitious symbol common in the Middle East called Hamsa (meaning five as in five fingers) which is an old-world amulet to ward off the Evil Eye.

Mom then identified herself as Jewish to a curious woman with a Christian cross necklace. That lady then said: "I love the Jewish People." I was kind of stunned that there was even a need to say anything like that. It is as though we were being placated that it is OK to be Jewish and we are safe in the knowing that Christians "love" us. Since I knew her Christian motives, I understood her being "trained" to say it. I am also convinced that she was very honest in saying it. But why even say anything like that?

That trend is a narrative by Christians that are trained to think that Jews are the needed vehicle for the Second coming of Jesus Christ. In their eyes, Jews have to be "loved" and "protected" from all the evil doers or else "Jesus is not coming back." Unfortunately, it is condescending and treats Jews like pawns in their big scheme of things. I have not seen this type of "Jewish love" extended to other religions or people as a whole.

Basically, as a Jew, I either laugh at these statements, ignore them, or depending on the speaker, I would engage them in discussion or conversation.

Another interesting Anti-Jewish experience I was only tangentially aware of, was the revelation in 1994 that the Church of Jesus Christ of Latter-day Saints, also known as the Mormon or LDS church decided to secretly baptize by proxy (convert) Jews murdered during the holocaust (and others as well).[1-4] Was I shocked? Not at all! But it showed the arrogance and doctrine of conversion at all cost. Really? Convert murdered dead people? Dead people have no choice! Why convert them? Isn't it enough that the LDS church actively seek to convert anyone to their version of religion via a worldwide missionary activity? Do they need to desecrate the Jewish dead as well? I now took it personally! They, in their deeds, "converted" members of my murdered relatives! The Church leadership backed off (sort of) in 1995 by agreement with protesting Jewish organizations stating they will limit this practice to only Mormon ancestry. That statement is hollow as no one was a Mormon prior to their religion being formed in 1830 in New York State. This practice of paper baptism still continues under other means and guises.

Final thought

As much as I think rational people are involved, there is no changing the hearts and minds of zealots!

> Jews do not want to be part of other's religion.
> Do not convert us!
> Do not save us!
> Do not resurrect us!
> Do not involve us in your deeds!
> Do not invoke us in your politics!
> Do not involve us in your failures, disasters and biases!

Solve your own issues and don't blame us for everything that ails the society!

We are part of the global community and strive to help (Tikun Olam). We have no "space laser" that started forest fires in the Western US and we do not control the world.

I and many Jews recognize this will fall on deaf ears.

PART IX: COMMENTS

CHAPTER 28

Closing Comments

This book, has taken the reader through our collective human experience from pre historic days to today. The Topic of hate was studied. A further emphasis on religious institutions in the realm of hate were discussed. I showed specifics examples of how Christianity started from its beginning with a collective blaming of Jews. Same examination with Islam role in trying to "fix" the wrong doings of what they consider "bad" Jews. Then there is extensive reviews of newer forms of Anti-Semitism and hate. Then you saw the various manifestations and media forms used to spread the hate. You saw my personal experiences and finally my closing comments on that topic.

Summary

The twentieth century was a century of change in relationship to Jews specifically after World War Two. There is an understanding from some Christian leadership regarding Jews and the blaming of an entire people by those interpreting the New Testament. Evangelical Christians consider Anti-Semitism is "un-Christian" and wrong." The Church of England as well as the Pope in Rome came out with statements of support. None of those separates Jews from being looked at as a commodity to be converted to Christianity at a later date. Jews are not free from bigoted Anti-Semitism.

To Christians, there is always a subtle reminder that Jews sinned, but that they did not know why or that God did not reveal to them his intentions. Thus, they are to be "forgiven" (notice that the intent here is for all Jews, not just the ones present during the crucifixion to be forgiven). As though I and my fellow Jewish people need forgiveness for something we were not involved in, but are lumped by association to texts written by unknowns 2,000 some odd years ago. But, at the "end of time" or the "second coming of their messiah," Jews are a means to that end. That end is that Jews will accept Jesus as their savior or else it will not occur. That acceptance is conversion, and is their "logical" and necessary ingredient to Christianity's ultimate goal.

In an ideal world, Christians would modify their texts written by the early converts of the first and second century and remove statements from the gospels pertaining to collective guilt and God's punishment for the entire Jewish population forever. Secondly, there is a need to separate Jews from Christian ideology. We are not your commodity nor are we the means to your ultimate journey in life (or after life). We are not in your way, nor are we to be your enablers!

The reality is clear! this will never happen because zealots or manipulators wrote the texts and created that vengeful narrative which is repeated now for 2000 years. It will not change, because going against that narrative will cause a rift in the various Christian communities and there is no value in it since it will run counter to the teachings being ministered. Christianity and Islam are both proselyting religions where missionaries are the cornerstones of those institutions. Not converting Jews is not an option for them.

The cycle of hate cannot be broken. It can only be minimized by education and open mindedness. It must be in the forefront of any society to try to eliminate or minimize hate and hate crimes.

In the USA, we have a situation in which hate is proliferated, disseminated and tolerated under the First amendment of the US Constitution, "Free Speech." That is an abuse of the original intent in which free speech was designed to protect the common citizen from state oppression/persecution and abuse of power (like the King of England). It was never meant as a vehicle to disparage and verbally abuse each other. As long as there is a blanket approval for any speech and especially by means of power centers (and now the internet), hate, Anti-Semitism and racism will continue. There is no point in pressing the Free speech curtailment since it is part and parcel of the US culture and is accepted in many Western countries as well. The next step is to counter with sensible speech and pointing out the sources and bigotry that prevails.

CHAPTER 29

The Solution is Education (but only partially)

There is always a tendency to jump to the fixes. And I must admit, I too have been there with the thinking that education is the key. Yes, education is an ingredient, but there needs to be more. Will there ever be a "cure" for hate? The simple answer is NO. Why? Because it is genetically engrained in every living being to fear and the basic need for self-preservation. Therefore, people will always be on alert to threats. There are real threats and then there are perceived threats. Real threat is one in which there is a physical attack or verbal attack. Threats and hate also manifest themselves via acts that are economical in nature. And then there are perceived threats. You will hear that for example that there is a war on Christianity, or that Jews manipulate banking, media, entertainment and thus pollute the mind, body and soul of innocent folks. Humans act upon what we are experiencing, taught, indoctrinated, or the company we keep. Because humans are pre disposed to follow. There will always be the element of being manipulated toward hate and some act upon those perceived or fabricated threats.

Now what? How do we go beyond the prime source of hate specifically toward Jews? How do we convey the message to those interpreting anti-Jewish writings in religious Christian and Muslim texts? How can a message of tolerance and openness be conveyed?

If you are reading this book and got to this chapter, then you already know that both Christianity and Islam have texts attacking Jews for wrong doings. It then gets translated to action by many in which Jews have been blamed for practically every ill and disaster that befell those believers.

The written words are engrained and are part and parcel of the New

Testament and Quran. There is no rewriting or correcting those to reflect modern times and sensibilities. What is written cannot be unwritten (or can it?). An educational process must accompany any and all those writings. In addition, at religious institutions, teachers must not be Anti-Semitics or convey literal interpretations of the old writings. The Ancients did not see the world as is today. Sensibilities thousands of years ago are not to be repeated today. Slavery and subjugation so common back then have no place today anywhere. Human or animal sacrifices have no place today nor ever. Following a text in which a writer invokes the "wrath of God" is not to be followed or taken as a command. Vigorous condemnation followed up by a disciplined approach to teaching needs to be in place. For example: It is not enough for the Pope to condemn Jewish persecution. There has to be some educational component to it.

- **Our job as humans** is to treat each other without collective malice.

- **Our job as educators** is to proliferate the message that collective guilt is old world teaching and is wrong on its face and manifestation.

- **Our job as educators** is to provide meaning as to why those writings were written as such.

- **Our job as Jewish people** is to bring this form of hate to the surface by discussing it in the open.

- **Our job as Jewish people** is to let the young children know that these persecutions did occur, and not fall into denial and historical revisionism that the Holocaust never happened or was not that bad.

- **Our job as open-minded individuals** is to let everyone know that there are NO fine racists. Former president Donald Trump in his initial response to the violent protests in Charlottesville, Virginia in 2017 said "there are fine people on both sides.

- **Our job is to push back on hate speech.** When you hear things like "Jews will not replace us" as in Charlottesville white supremacist (Unite the Right) in March in 2017. It is a responsibility of every person to condemn it.

Reality:

I know full well that those pointers will not be fully implemented by everyone involved, and even if they are, it will not change the minds of those with ill intent. I advocate education only because doing nothing will simply aggravate conditions. Legal consequences should be left to the authorities which will reflect on how those societies want to lead their lives. Only by knowing that we are all humans regardless of our differences and beliefs, will we be just! Fear is not a substitute for cooperation. Know that fear only closes the doors and makes everyone a perceived enemy.

Lastly, unlike previous times since our expulsion as Jews from Israel (Judea) by the Romans 2000 years ago, we now have a land where Jews, Muslim and Christians of all kinds and denominations can have a safe place to live, prosper and be equal part of the world population. Those that want to create a wedge between Jews and Israel are just confusing matters and want to continue the chaos.

Jews cannot be separated from Israel even if many Jews do not live in Israel nor identify with its politics. Being Jewish is not only a religion, but a people. We are called "Am Israel" in Hebrew (people of Israel). Since Jews mostly live in a diaspora, many have no intentions to emigrate or "return" to the land of Israel, the fact that they identify themselves as Jews gives them the connection to the land of Israel even if one is not a practicing Jew.

That is our connection.

When modern Israel ceases to exist, Anti-Semitic acts like the Holocaust will reemerge.

There is another form of Anti-Jewish, Anti-Zionist, Anti-Israel movement that is a direct result of the creation of Israel in 1948. The narrative that is perpetuated is that Jews have no rights to the land and unless they leave, they will all be slaughtered and thrown to the sea (Arab statements).

Thus, until and when that Arab-Israeli conflict is resolved, acts against Jews as a collective punishment (what else is new in Anti-Jewish sentiments) will continue and amplify each and every time there is fighting going on in the region. Jews that have nothing to do with Israel are attacked for what is going on in the Middle-East. You see it routinely! In May 2021 when primarily liberal minded individuals were quick to condemn Israel retaliation against Hamas launching thousands of rockets from Gaza strip saying how unfair Israel was. It then triggered an "open Season" against any and all Jews. Is there a solution here? Will there ever be a reduction of violence? Unfortunately, no! And the prime reason is religion! It is the great separator. I do not see a resolution to the Arab Israeli situation as long as there is no tolerance for co-existence. Unfortunately, the middle East has always been a hot bed of violence. Empires always love going through that area and exploit the division of the local populations, manipulating them to their advantage and perpetuating discourse. Modern times did not infuse tolerance as people still fighting amongst themselves along tribal, ethnic and religious lines. Peace is only measured as a cessation of hostilities for a while, only to flare up into major and minor conflicts. Democracy amongst Arabs in the middle east does not seem to work. Either there is a secular or a religious dictatorship. And when there is an attempt in democratic elections, the outcome is always violence as in Egypt's election of the Islamic Brotherhood's president Mohamed Morsi, ending in his ouster by a military coup d'état a year later. Another example is the takeover by force of the Gaza strip by a brutal organization (Hamas) in 2007. The Middle East is replete with conflicts. Even organizations like ISIS (Daesh) that terrorized Iraq and Syria were intolerant to any other version of Islam other than theirs. Continuation of Islamic religious schools (madrasas) teaching extreme violence and intolerance is prevalent and ongoing. There are millions of young minds that go through these training grounds and then become susceptible to intolerance toward non-Muslims, acts of hate, violence, wars, destructions. . . . I really do not see a stop to this and that leads me to the conclusion that hate actions are a learned attribute. As long as one learns to hate, there will be no end to it!

NOTES AND REFERENCES

Chapter 1: Why Hate

I decided that a starting point to the study of any hate is to look at humans and what makes us tick. What are the basics that make us all fear?

Chapter 2: Why Loyalty

Loyalty is a prime ingredient to any organization. Here I where it is built upon our fears and desires as humans.

1. Dreyfus affair. Wikipedia
   https://en.wikipedia.org/wiki/Dreyfus_affair

Chapter 3: Sacrifice

There is always a price to pay. Fear, loyalty demands it.

Chapter 4: Systems of Conformity

1. Mel Brooks movie
   https://www.youtube.com/watch?v=pEAXGY_HFU0&ab_channel=havelhavalim1

Chapter 5: Religion as Forms of Institutions

Religions are the cement that allows fear, hate, worship and organized forms of institutionalizing them.

Chapter 6: The Role of Religion in Hate

1. Jewish space lasers
   https://en.wikipedia.org/wiki/Marjorie_Taylor_Greene#Camp_Fire_conspiracy_theory
2. 5000 gods, Ricky Gervais Twitter
   https://twitter.com/rickygervais/status/681785157808992256
3. Abraham in the book of Exodus
   https://en.wikipedia.org/wiki/Abraham
4. Untermench
   https://en.wikipedia.org/wiki/Untermensch
5. Covid misinformation and blaming the Jews
   https://en.wikipedia.org/wiki/COVID-19_misinformation
   https://en.wikipedia.org/wiki/Neturei_Karta

Chapter 7: Early Christianity

1. Greek language used in the New Testament writing
   https://en.wikipedia.org/wiki/Language_of_the_New_Testament
2. Maccabees resistance
   https://en.wikipedia.org/wiki/Maccabees

Chapter 8: The Islamic World and Jews

1. Arab Anti-Jewish/Semitism

   https://en.wikipedia.org/wiki/Antisemitism_in_the_Arab_world

2. Slaughter the Jews

   https://instablogs.com/itbah-al-yahud-or-khaybar-ya-yahood.html

3. badges

   https://www.yadvashem.org/artifacts/featured/Jewish-badges.html

4. "protection" fee (Jizyah)

   https://en.wikipedia.org/wiki/Jizya

5. Treatment of Non-Jews in Muslim lands

   https://katz.sas.upenn.edu/resources/blog/what-do-you-know-dhimmi-jewish-legal-status-under-muslim-rule

6. Book The Dhimmi: Jews and Christians Under Islam. Bat Ye'or author, 1985

Chapter 9: Biblical Jews

Jews today are not the same as those in the bible.

Chapter 10: Who is a Jew?

The great debate and the tool to separate, segregate and harm Jews.

1. Clothing

   https://en.wikipedia.org/wiki/Jewish_religious_clothing

2. In an interview with New York Magazine, Rudy Giuliani says he is "more of a Jew" than George Soros, who is a Holocaust survivor. CNN

   Dec 24, 2019 story

   http://nymag.com/intelligencer/2019/12/a-conversation-with-rudy-giuliani-over-bloody-marys.html

3. why Soros is being used for Anti-Semitism

   https://www.adl.org/blog/the-anti-semitism-lurking-behind-george-soros-conspiracy-theories

4. Conversos

   https://www.jewishvirtuallibrary.org/marranos-conversos-and-new-christians

5. Jews

   https://urj.org/who-we-are/history

6. Ben Shapiro on real Jews

   Shapiro is editor in chief of The Daily Wire, a conservative website. In 2010, he reportedly called Rahm Emanuel, the mayor of Chicago who was a chief of staff under President Bill Clinton, and the liberal Hungarian-American billionaire George Soros "kapos," in reference to Jews who aided Nazis during the Holocaust

   Shapiro describes himself as a devout Orthodox Jew, this has never stopped him from shaming other members of the Jewish faith. He has claimed that only Orthodox Jews know what it means to be Jewish, and that all Jews who criticize the Israeli government are self-loathing. He has attacked Jews who support progressive American politics, labeling us as "JINOs" or "Jews in name only."

https://www.imdb.com/title/tt9356966/?ref_=ttrel_rel_tt

Rebuttal Boston Globe https://www.bostonglobe.com/2020/01/15/opinion/bad-jews/

- The Jewish people has always been plagued by Bad Jews, who undermine it from within. In America, those Bad Jews largely vote Democrat.
- 9:48 AM · Nov 8, 2011·Twitter Web Client

7. Anne Coulter perfected Jews

"COULTER: No, we think — we just want Jews to be perfected, as they say."

https://www.youtube.com/watch?v=2wnPHFSdrME

http://opiniojuris.org/2007/10/10/ann-coulter-christians-are-perfected-jews/

8. Nuremberg laws

https://en.wikipedia.org/wiki/Nuremberg_Laws

Chapter 11: The Age of Enlightenment

Blind obedience makes way to science, pseudo-science and junk science.

1. Age of Enlightenment

https://www.history.com/topics/british-history/enlightenment

2. Eugenics

https://en.wikipedia.org/wiki/Eugenics

https://en.wikipedia.org/wiki/Nazi_eugenics

Chapter 12: Anti-Semitism, how did it start?

1. Spanish Inquisition

https://www.catholiceducation.org/en/controversy/the-inquisition/the-truth-about-the-spanish-inquisition.html

https://en.wikipedia.org/wiki/Tom%C3%A1s_de_Torquemada

2. Body of Christ

John 6:53–57, Jesus says, "Very truly I tell you, unless you eat the flesh of the Son of Man and drink his blood, you have no life in you. Whoever eats my flesh and drinks my blood has eternal life, and I will raise them up at the last day. For my flesh is real food and my blood is real drink. Whoever eats my flesh and drinks my blood remains in me, and I in them. Just as the living Father sent me and I live because of the Father, so the one who feeds on me will live because of me. This is the bread that came down from heaven. Your ancestors ate manna and died, but whoever feeds on this bread will live forever." Upon hearing these words, many of Jesus' followers said, "This is a hard teaching" (verse 60), and many of them actually stopped following Him that day (verse 66).

Chapter 13: Anti-Semitism, The New Age.

1. Gottingen school of history

https://en.wikipedia.org/wiki/G%C3%B6ttingen_school_of_history

2. Islam and Jews described as rebellious and animal like

Quran, in chapter 5, verses 59-60

Say, 'O Prophet,' "O People of the Book! Do you resent us only because we believe in Allah and what has been revealed to us and what was revealed before—while most of you are rebellious?"

Say, 'O Prophet,' "Shall I inform you of those who deserve a worse punishment from Allah 'than the rebellious'? It is those who earned Allah's condemnation and displeasure—some being reduced to apes and pigs and worshippers of false gods. These are far worse in rank and farther astray from the Right Way."

3. After WW1 Arab Anti Semitism

https://en.wikipedia.org/wiki/Antisemitism_in_the_Arab_world

4. Code Pink

https://en.wikipedia.org/wiki/Code_Pink

Chapter 14: British Anti-Semitism

An example of Soft Anti-Semitism, and the paradox of Christian Zionism

1. Russian revolution

https://en.wikipedia.org/wiki/Russian_Revolution

2. World Zionist Congress

https://en.wikipedia.org/wiki/World_Zionist_Congress

3. Balfour declaration

https://en.wikipedia.org/wiki/Balfour_Declaration

4. Anti Semitism in the United Kingdom

https://en.wikipedia.org/wiki/Antisemitism_in_the_United_Kingdom

5. British Zionism

https://en.wikipedia.org/wiki/Christian_Zionism_in_the_United_Kingdom

6. Christian Anti-Semitism

https://www.jta.org/quick-reads - link not available, but here is the text

Church of England says centuries of Christian anti-Semitism led to the Holocaust

NOVEMBER 25, 2019 2:28 PM

(JTA) — Centuries of Christian anti-Semitism led to the Holocaust, the Church of England said in a new report that called for repentance.

"God's Unfailing Word: Theological and Practical Perspectives on Christian-Jewish Relations," which was released last week, also asked Christians to accept the importance of Zionism for most Jews.

The report, more than 140 pages, calls the Christian-Jewish relationship "a gift of God to the Church, to be received with care, respect and gratitude, so that we may learn more fully about God's purposes for us and all the world."

British Chief Rabbi Ephraim Mirvis criticized the report, however, and in an afterword to the document wrote that it fails to reject targeting Jews for conversion.

7. Christian Zionism

https://en.wikipedia.org/wiki/Christian_Zionism

8. UK rabbi

https://www.itv.com/news/2019-11-25/chief-rabbi-warns-soul-of-nation-is-at-stake-if-labour-wins-general-election/?fbclid=IwAR3d9X9ukKckbQ734xQkN7enUjpX1vpOmEFtDuwwv3zPOUW5tMqxx0sqPyE

9. Rebuttal

https://voxpoliticalonline.com/2019/11/27/unafraid-Jews-respond-to-chief-rabbis-and-

other-claims-that-they-fear-a-corbyn-labour-government/?fbclid=IwAR2jKAc3qhpY-cUt7_
Fh4kuz_RmATY8JgnI1dYway_RQikJt2EeXerAqQbw

10. Jeremy Corbyn

   https://en.wikipedia.org/wiki/Jeremy_Corbyn

Chapter 15: Current Anti-Semitism

Another big wave is coming. Anti Semites, Anti-Jewish actors are in the open again.

1. The term Repug- slang term for Republicans

   https://www.urbandictionary.com/define.php?term=repug

2. Ben Shapiro on Jewish leftist.

   Example: https://www.youtube.com/watch?v=M5IqH7oJ9h4

3. Republican candidate on hanging opponent

   https://www.rollingstone.com/t/danielle-stella/

4. Rick Wiles

   https://www.snopes.com/fact-check/rick-wiles-trump-
   impeachment/?fbclid=IwAR3w0Tfnt-TJVhaO0Wb0LkHEEvfI0NYzvjgDDmOYNMA0VQ4b
   V4KaIXzOrPc

5. Al Jazira on Jewish porn

   https://www.memri.org/tv/jazeera-internet-midan-voice-jews-created-porn-industry-
   pollute-american-christian-values

   Al-Jazeera's Midan Voice Internet Channel: Jews Created and Control the Porn Industry in
   Order to Pollute American and Christian Values

   #7564 | 03:58

   Source: The Internet - "Al-Jazeera's Midan Voice Online Audio Channel (Qatar)"

   On October 29, 2019, a video about Jewish control of the pornography industry was uploaded
   by Midan Voice, an Al-Jazeera Internet audio channel directed at youth. The narrator said
   that the Jews dominate the porn industry and spread pornography in order to "pollute
   Christian culture" and destroy American values. Midan Voice was launched on YouTube and
   Soundcloud in January 2018.

Chapter 16: Atheism and Jews

Even those with no stated religions are jumping on the bandwagon of hate.

1. Noah's arc

   https://en.wikipedia.org/wiki/Noah%27s_Ark

2. Flood myth

   https://en.wikipedia.org/wiki/Flood_myth

3. Leon Trotsky

   https://en.wikipedia.org/wiki/Leon_Trotsky

4. Communist party

   https://en.wikipedia.org/wiki/Communism

5. Karl Marx

   https://en.wikipedia.org/wiki/Karl_Marx

6. Ghetto

   https://en.wikipedia.org/wiki/Ghetto

7. Treaty of Versailles

   https://www.history.com/topics/world-war-i/treaty-of-versailles-1

8. Atheism

   https://en.wikipedia.org/wiki/Atheism

9. Armageddon

   https://en.wikipedia.org/wiki/Tel_Megiddo

Chapter 17: Conversion, Missionaries and Proselytizing

Jews are a prime target for conversion. Just leave us alone please!

1. Korean Christian trying to convert Jews in Jerusalem.

   https://www.youtube.com/watch?v=myKv-vz_KAI&t=25s

2. Syngman Rhee

   https://en.wikipedia.org/wiki/Syngman_Rhee

3. Unification church

   https://en.wikipedia.org/wiki/Unification_Church

4. New Testament- Matthew on Jews guilt of Jesus killing:

   Matthew 27:24-25

   Revised Standard Version

   Pilate Hands Jesus over to Be Crucified

   24 So when Pilate saw that he was gaining nothing, but rather that a riot was beginning, he took water and washed his hands before the crowd, saying, "I am innocent of this man's blood; [a] see to it yourselves." 25 And all the people answered, "His blood be on us and on our children!"

5. Anne Frank diary quote:

   "I can shake off everything as I write; my sorrows disappear, my courage is reborn." "I've found that there is always some beauty left—in nature, sunshine, freedom, in yourself; these can all help you." "No one has ever become poor by giving." "I don't think of all the misery, but of the beauty that still remains."

   'I still believe, in spite of everything, that people are truly good at heart.' On 15 July 1944, Anne Frank wrote one of her most inspiring quotes.

Chapter 18: The Holocaust

Institutionalized murder machine unleashes its hate in an unprecedented evil.

1. Nazi party

   https://en.wikipedia.org/wiki/Nazi_Party

2. Wilhelm Gustloff

   https://en.wikipedia.org/wiki/Wilhelm_Gustloff

3. Protocols of the Elders of Zion

   https://en.wikipedia.org/wiki/The_Protocols_of_the_Elders_of_Zion

4. Usury

   https://en.wikipedia.org/wiki/Usury

5. Xenophobia

   https://en.wikipedia.org/wiki/Xenophobia

6. Reichstag fire

   https://en.wikipedia.org/wiki/Reichstag_fire

7. Nuremberg Laws of 1935

   https://en.wikipedia.org/wiki/Nuremberg_Laws

8. Kristallnacht

   https://en.wikipedia.org/wiki/Kristallnacht

9. Vatican complicity and silence of Jews murdered by Nazis

   https://www.npr.org/2020/08/29/907076135/records-from-once-secret-archive-offer-new-clues-into-vatican-response-to-holoca

10. Holocaust Anti-Semitism

    https://www.yadvashem.org/holocaust/holocaust-antisemitism.html

11. Genocide

    https://www.yadvashem.org/holocaust/holocaust-antisemitism/terms-genocide.html

12. Concentration camps

    https://en.wikipedia.org/wiki/Internment

Chapter 19: Zionism and the Return of Jews to Israel

The eternal Jewish desire to return to the land of Israel.

1. Madagascar plan

   https://en.wikipedia.org/wiki/Proposals_for_a_Jewish_state#Madagascar_plan

2. Mandate for Palestine

   https://en.wikipedia.org/wiki/Mandate_for_Palestine

3. Lawrence of Arabia

   https://en.wikipedia.org/wiki/T._E._Lawrence

4. Balfour Declaration

   https://en.wikipedia.org/wiki/Balfour_Declaration

5. Second Aliyah

   https://en.wikipedia.org/wiki/Second_Aliyah

6. Kibutz

   https://en.wikipedia.org/wiki/Kibbutz

7. Zionism

   https://www.britannica.com/topic/Zionism

8. Partition

   https://en.wikipedia.org/wiki/United_Nations_Partition_Plan_for_Palestine

9. Neturei karta

   https://en.wikipedia.org/wiki/Neturei_Karta

10. Palestinian solidarity

    (https://en.wikipedia.org/wiki/Palestine_Solidarity_Movement)

11. Sympathizers

    https://www.reddit.com/r/DebateReligion/comments/4d6pn5/is_atheism_also_antisemitism_xpost_from_ratheism/

12. Zionism

    https://www.timesofisrael.com/epic-historical-novel-digs-deep-into-zionisms-less-probed-western-european-roots/

13. Jizya

    https://en.wikipedia.org/wiki/Jizya

14. ISIS, Daesh, ISIL

    https://en.wikipedia.org/wiki/Islamic_State

Chapter 20: After the War Anti-Semitism

Not everything is "Quiet on the Western Front" The hate continues.

1. Kielce pogrom

    https://www.smithsonianmag.com/history/kielce-post-holocaust-pogrom-poland-still-fighting-over-180967681/

2. Polish historian Jan T. Gross in his 2006 book *Fear: Anti-Semitism in Poland After Auschwitz.*

    https://www.amazon.com/Fear-Anti-Semitism-Poland-After-Auschwitz/dp/0812967461

3. Post war pogroms

    https://www.smithsonianmag.com/history/kielce-post-holocaust-pogrom-poland-still-fighting-over-180967681/#Yk3T7yCiybY0pMpE.99

4. https://www.yadvashem.org/articles/general/anti-Jewish-violence-in-poland-after-liberation.html

Chapter 21: Deniers and Revisionists

The narratives of erasing Jews with bogus facts and spinning events.

1. https://en.wikipedia.org/wiki/Antisemitism_in_Islam

2. http://bibleodyssey.org/tools/bible-basics/is-the-new-testament-anti-Jewish

Chapter 22: The New Reality in the USA

1. White Christian terrorists

    https://www.universiteitleiden.nl/binaries/content/assets/customsites/perspectives-on-terrorism/2020/issue-5/benam-and-weimann.pdf

2. Reference from Time magazine:

    BY OLIVIA B. WAXMAN

    JANUARY 25, 2021 12:04 PM EST

    Among the most shocking images from the Jan. 6 insurrection on Capitol Hill were pictures of a man wearing a sweatshirt that said "Camp Auschwitz" and "work brings freedom." It's an anti-Semitic reference to the Nazi concentration camp and extermination center where over 1 million Jewish people died or were murdered during the Holocaust.

    Whole article here: https://time.com/5932489/white-supremacy-holocaust-nazi-history-capitol-attack/?fbclid=IwAR3rbFxnAhrmX70yhd2CwDhio_lmIMPGQeIHkWsa_fQbJSl-7KbeaeA8ZS0

3. The newest vehicle for the oldest hatred: OPINION

   Social media is just the latest way to sow hatred of Jewish people.

   By Pamela Paresky and John Farmer

   January 29, 2021, 6:00 AM

   • 9 min read

   https://abcnews.go.com/Politics/newest-vehicle-oldest-hatred-opinion/
   story?id=75542375&cid=clicksource_4380645_6_three_posts_card_hed

4. Tikun Olam

   https://www.jpost.com/opinion/the-art-of-tikkun-olam-creating-to-heal-the-
   world-585801

5. Muslim Uyghurs in China

   (https://en.wikipedia.org/wiki/Uyghurs

6. Pinkwashing

   https://www.aljazeera.com/opinions/2014/8/9/against-the-pinkwashing-of-israel

Chapter 23: Sports, Hate and Anti-Semitism

1. https://www.adl.org/resources/blog/antisemitism-european-soccer-rise

2. Polish Soccer Fans Call for The Burning of Jews

   https://www.jpost.com/diaspora/polish-soccer-fans-torch-jewish-effigies-fly-banner-
   calling-for-burning-of-jews-466317

3. English soccer

   https://www.youtube.com/watch?v=tZjNcXzm3Qw

4. European Soccer Anti-Semitism Explodes

   Here is a review of a Dutch soccer team hooligans chants:

5. https://www.youtube.com/watch?v=5xT7Zo6XAVQ

6. https://www.youtube.com/watch?v=tHAqTIDuOKk

7. Belgium Soccer fans singing Anti-Semitic songs

   https://www.jta.org/2021/12/30/global/soccer-fans-filmed-singing-about-killing-jews-in-
   belgium

8. American Football player

   https://www.insider.com/desean-jackson-posts-anti-semitic-message-on-
   instagram-2020-7

Chapter 24: Hate in the Street

A collection of graffiti, defacing and toppling over Jewish headstones in cemeteries

Chapter 25: Words

The old saying of "Sticks and Stones will break my bones, but words never will" is just BS. Words can and do damage much more. They incite violence on large scale.

1. Donald Trump remarks to Jewish conference;

   https://www.whitehouse.gov/briefings-statements/remarks-president-trump-israeli-
   american-council-national-summit-2019/

   https://www.vanityfair.com/news/2019/12/donald-trump-anti-semitic-remarks

https://www.jpost.com/Opinion/Four-Things-that-should-concern-Israelis-from-Trumps-Speech-at-the-IAC-610570

"Inflaming Antisemitism – Trump referred to the event's audience of Israeli-Americans as "killer real-estate" agents, people with money who would support his presidency in order to avoid taxation. Even if Trump is expressing 'light' antisemitism, or if he admires these people because of these imagined characteristics, we still have a problem. Statements as such feed ever-increasing antisemitism in the US, generating anxiety in Jewish communities which until recently have felt secure. Statements like these simply add more fuel to an existing fire."

2. Jewess

https://www.heyalma.com/its-time-to-reclaim-the-word-jewess/

https://www.wordsense.eu/Jewes/

Chapter 26: Anti-Semitism in Movies

Some are fun to watch with popcorn, others are full of venom

Chapter 27: My Personal Experiences

A look thru my "soft experience" of Anti-Semitism and a look at the Holocaust thru the listening to my family's experiences.

Mormons converting dead Jews

1. https://www.avotaynu.com/mormons/MormonAgreement.pdf
2. https://www.avotaynu.com/mormons/RadkeyReportSummary.pdf
3. https://www.avotaynu.com/mormons/RadkeyReportDetail.pdf
4. https://www.jewishgen.org/infofiles/ldsagree.html?gclid=Cj0KCQiAnuGNBh
   CPARIsACbnLzrSGBFMxL4Ptf6GZRhK6OWEybw8YBqLMCtZZ6CJSG-ybw8SBTs-
   PP0aAmhOEALw_wcB

Chapter 28: Closing Comments

Let's wrap it up.

Chapter 29: The Solution is Education

Is there a real solution to Anti-Semitism? Most likely no.

ANTI-SEMITIC ORGANIZATIONS

KKK

This is a white Christian only organization primarily in the south of the USA that advocate Christian white people only purity. They see the Jews and black folks as the obstacle to their aim of a white Christian USA as a country.

Proud Boys

A relatively new organization that espouses the same as the KKK in its aim, but also is anti-liberal group that advocates their version of society.

Aryan nation and Nazi groups

These are similar to the KKK, and advocate not only white supremacy, but a specific version of whites that the Nazi party in pre and during WW2 selected as the pure master race.

Nation of Islam

Notorious black leader obsessed about Jews being the root of all evil. Black converts to Islam that are subjugated to a single leader advocating destruction of Jews.

Black Hebrew Israelites (they believe that they are the true decedents). The group is relatively new phenomena and was created in the 1800 as part of a "revelation from God" in which African Americans are the true decedents of the original Hebrews. However, there is a fringe element of this movement that is racists and promotes Black supremacy over whites. This is an active hate organization (New Jersey shooting Dec 10, 2019. Murder of innocent Jews in grocery store)

This is a group that goes out of its way of spreading a narrative that they are the "true Jews" and the white Jews are not. So regardless of the definition, they execute their narrative thru acts of violence as was demonstrated in New Jersey in 2019.

Indirect Anti-Jewish organizations

A recent visible side effect of not directly Anti-Jewish or Anti-Semitic rhetoric and action is the infiltration or leadership of social justice organizations by these individuals.

Of interest are the many progressive movement leaders like at the Women March who are interwoven to organization of hate. They refuse to disassociate themselves of overtly racist and divisive organization while touting the women right movements. They are associated or support the Nation of Islam or the Anti-Israel BDS movement, or anti-Zionist concept they associate with Israel.

Another recent phenomenon is the QAnon movement. This is a conspiracy laden loose social media with no structure. It is a Right wing inspired movement in which "anything that they throw against the wall" sticks with weak minded minions that would subscribe to anything they dislike. Specifically, to Anti-Jewish rhetoric is their "Jewish Space lasers" starting wild fires and the century long cry that the Rothchild's continue to manipulate world democracy.

Whenever someone or some organization takes possession of their version of absolute truth (as though it justifies violence) and is one sided in their zeal both verbal and in deeds, it invites acts of hate and violence.

My Comment

It is up to any Human rights or social justice organization to distance their message and messengers from hateful venues. You can't be pro women advocate and at the same time be Anti-Jewish, Anti-Israel, Anti-Zionist, Anti-Semitic and claim to fight for the cause of women equality. The two are not related!

www.ingramcontent.com/pod-product-compliance
Lightning Source LLC
Chambersburg PA
CBHW080403270326
41927CB00015B/3337